M000206736

Religious Vows,
the Sermon on the Mount,
and Christian Living

Bonnie B. Thurston

LITURGICAL PRESS
Collegeville, Minnesota

www.litpress.org

Cover design by Joachim Rhoades, O.S.B.

1	2	3	4	5	6	7	8

Library of Congress Cataloging-in-Publication Data

Thurston, Bonnie Bowman.
  Religious vows, the Sermon on the mount, and Christian living / Bonnie B. Thurston.
    p. cm.
  Summary: "Insights into living for all Christians is forthcoming through a contemporary understanding of religious vows and the the Gospel of Matthew's Sermon on the mount"—Provided by publisher.
  Includes bibliographical references.
  ISBN-13: 978-0-8146-2929-1 (pbk. : alk. paper)
  ISBN-10: 0-8146-2929-6 (pbk. : alk. paper)
  1. Christian life. 2. Sermon on the mount. 3. Vows. I. Title.

BV4501.3.T52 2006
241.5'3—dc22   2005011787

*In gratitude for the friendship of the Daughters of Wisdom
of the Province of Great Britain and Ireland,
living and among the Great Cloud of Witnesses*

Contents

Introduction 1

Abbreviations 6

Chapter 1
The Beatitudes: Blessings for a New Life:
   Matthew 5:1-12 7

Chapter 2
The Kingdom Calls for Charity:
   Matthew 5:13-16, 27-30, 43-48 32

Chapter 3
The Kingdom Calls for Detachment:
   Matthew 6:19-34 47

Chapter 4
The Kingdom Calls for Humility:
   Matthew 6:10; 7:1-5, 12, 13-14 65

Chapter 5
Monasticism and Marriage 81

Appendix 100

Introduction

Let me begin with a word about the genesis of this material. In June 2003 I had a letter from a friend who is a Daughter of Wisdom in the Province of Great Britain and Ireland saying "At our last meeting we made a plan for 2004 to study and reflect on vows and renewal of religious life. We wondered if you could give us some biblical background on the subject." Being who I am, I asked for some clarification. Sister replied "At our last chapter meeting of the Province, two years ago, sisters expressed a strong desire to have a new look at the vows. As they stand, Poverty, Chastity, and Obedience conjure up dry, tired, and outmoded memories of Religious Life, but they do not sum up Gospel living for us. . . . What we were hoping for is some biblical background on how Jesus lived the evangelical counsels as he proclaimed his kingdom—how he related to his Father, to himself, and to those he met—vis-à-vis the social, political, and religious lives of his day." As I thought about this request, I asked myself the question: "where does Jesus most clearly speak about Gospel living?" And that was an easy question. Clearly the Sermon on the Mount in Matthew's gospel is as good a summary of Jesus' teaching as we have. In fact, ". . . the literary genre of the Sermon on the Mount is that of an epitome presenting the theology of Jesus in a systematic fashion."[1] So the Sermon on the Mount provided the textual basis of the talks I was to give the

[1] Hans Dieter Betz, *Essays on the Sermon on the Mount* (Philadelphia: Fortress, 1985) 15.

1

Daughters of Wisdom in the Spring of 2004 and those talks are the substance of this book.

Equally clearly, it seems to me that the Beatitudes are a summary of Jesus' expectations for his followers. In the United States, particularly in the "Bible belt," we hear so much fuss about the 10 Commandments; oddly, some of us Christians don't seem to know the Beatitudes are our "marching orders." I suppose we could discuss, and certainly theologians in the history of the church *have* discussed, whether they are *praecepta*, basic rules of life for all Christians, or *consilia*, a demand for more and intended for those who want perfection. That they summarize Jesus' thinking, no one much disputes.

So that made the subject of the first chapter evident. This chapter is the most complex of the four because the Beatitudes are fundamental to how we envision our lives as Christians in the world. And their focus on the kingdom of heaven/God make it clear that Christian life has a public/political dimension by definition. The Beatitudes are frequently misinterpreted. They are seen in terms of personal piety but not in terms of public, and even political implication. So it is important to devote significant attention to them.

Then I was left with the matter of the "dry, tired, and outmoded" vows! That was somewhat harder. First, it has always seemed to me absurd to have people who aren't vowed and haven't lived them explaining vows to people who are and who have. Second, we now have the advantage of Sandra Schneiders' work on the vows and religious life, and one can't do better than that. So once again I asked myself a question: "What is the 'end' of each vow?" That is, "what Christian virtue or, more generally, spiritual attainment is each intended to nurture?" That was a very interesting thing to think about because it opened up the vows to the life of every serious Christian. In this connection I went back to a root exposition of monastic or religious vows in the modern Western church, the Rule of Benedict, and especially how what is found there applies to all Christians. Esther de Waal's *Seeking God: The Way of St. Benedict* is an incredibly helpful book in this regard.[2] What she did was to apply the Rule to her own life as the wife of a clergyman, mother of four sons, writer, and teacher, and then share her insights. You will encounter many of those insights in this little book.

Putting all this together, here is what I came up with: The vow of poverty is intended to detach us from the false values of a consumer and consuming society. Poverty is for Detachment. The vow of chastity is an invitation to go about the *whole* of life to reflect Gospel values, the most important of which, according to our Lord, is charity or love. To understand chastity only in terms of sexual expression is to misunderstand its intent. Chastity is for Charity. The vow of obedience is, in our day, perhaps the most profoundly countercultural because it asks us to take ourselves off center stage in our lives to point to something other than ourselves. Again, obedience characterized the life of Jesus, who spoke of himself as "gentle and humble" (Matt 11:29). We will need to define what humility means for psychologically healthy women (and men) in our day. But still, Obedience is for Humility. In fact, I think these formulations are very much in line with Louis Bouyer's classic understanding that the vows are for greater freedom: "Poverty . . . makes us free with regard to the world. Charity makes us free with regard to the flesh. Obedience makes us free with regard to our will itself and its basic egoism."[3]

With these ideas in mind, I went back to the Sermon on the Mount and discovered that significant portions of the Sermon addressed these very issues. And so the following four units of material evolved:

The Beatitudes: Blessings for a New Life (Matt 5:2-12)
The Kingdom Calls for Charity (Matt 5:13-16, 27-30, 43-48)
The Kingdom Calls for Detachment (Matt 6:19-34)

---

[2] Esther de Waal, *Seeking God: The Way of St. Benedict* (Collegeville: Liturgical Press, 1984).

[3] Louis Bouyer, *Introduction to Spirituality,* trans. Mary Perkins Ryan (New York: Desclee, 1961) 135.

The Kingdom Calls for Humility (Matt 6:10; 7:1-5, 12, 13-14)

The first chapter is a study on the Beatitudes that also introduces the very important matter of what Jesus meant by "kingdom of heaven/God." The other chapters begin with the relevant Bible passages and then move into the implications of each idea for the "social, political, and religious lives" of *our* day. Each chapter ends with a series of questions that can be used as discussion starters for groups or "points to ponder" for individuals. As I was preparing the talks I collected "versions" of the Beatitudes, and after the talks at the various venues the sisters shared with me "versions" they knew. I have included those in an appendix.

So let us begin with a quotation from Esther de Waal's *Seeking God*. She is speaking about the place of Scripture in the life of monastics . . . and of all of us:

> The "cry" of Scripture is perceived as the voice, the call of God. When the call is heard it must be embraced as a personal message with its living demands addressed to each individual. God's Word is not something static, past and dead; something lying inert between the covers of a book. It is what it is called: the manifestation of a living person whom one recognizes by the tone of voice. The call is not simply something out of a distant past; it comes today and comes to elicit a response from us and to engage us in dialogue.[4]

I hope the material that follows will both call forth a response in you and continue our dialogue with God and with each other.

I am deeply grateful for my ten years of association with the Daughters of Wisdom of Great Britain and Ireland, which began with my friendship with Sr. Eileen Catterson, D.W. and M.D., and especially for their invitation to speak to their community in the spring of 2004 on the theme "Wisdom Revisioning Religious

---

[4] de Waal, *Seeking God*, 33.

Life." Their positive response to this material led me to seek its publication. Their positive influence in my life has been significant. Special thanks to the communities in Lytham St. Anne's, Newcastle-on-Tyne, and Romsey for their wonderful hospitality.

Thanks also go to the community at Emmanuel School of Religion in Johnson City, Tennessee, where I was privileged to be Visiting Professor of Christian Spirituality for the fall 2004 semester and where I finished the work on this book.

Feast of All Saints 2004

Abbreviations

ABD   Anchor Bible Dictionary
LXX   Septuagint
NT   New Testament
NTS   New Testament Studies
OT   Old Testament
SM   Sermon on the Mount

The Beatitudes:
Blessings for a New Life

Matt 5:1-12

Introduction

The Sermon on the Mount begins with some of the best known and least understood verses in the New Testament, the Beatitudes, so called from the Vulgate's *beati,* "blessed." In coming to terms with them, as with the whole sermon, one must keep in mind the church to which they were first addressed. The evangelist we call Matthew was writing to address the needs of a growing church, and the material we call the Sermon on the Mount is a collection of Jesus' teachings. Its Hellenistic literary genre is the *epitome*, a condensation from a larger body of material made by an editor for a specific purpose. It is unusually brief and precise in style, and that style is poetic and proverbial. The Sermon on the Mount presents, in brief, the teaching of Jesus in a systematic fashion. As Hans Dieter Betz has written, "the text . . . sums up the uncompromising ethics of the historical Jesus."[1]

This "summary sermon" is carefully organized according to a pattern that would have been easily recognized by Jewish Christians in the second half of the first century. A Rabbinic proverb

---

[1] Hans Dieter Betz, "Sermon on the Mount" in David Noel Freedman et al., eds., *The Anchor Bible Dictionary* (New York: Doubleday, 1992) 5:1106.

stated, "By three things is the world sustained: by the Law, by the Temple service, and by deeds of loving kindness." Something like this seems to have provided Matthew with a structural principle for Jesus' first discourse (in a gospel that contains five discourses or sermons). After Matthew introduces the setting (5:1-2), Jesus pronounces eschatological blessings (5:3-12) on his disciples (5:13-17), and discusses Law (5:17-48), worship or piety (6:1-17), and various kinds of benevolent activity (6:19–7:23). The whole sermon is introduced by two deceptively simply verses.

In 5:1-2 we are told that there were crowds. The implication is that people are already following Jesus. What follows is a teaching for all to hear, a general summary, and admonition. It takes place on a mountain, with all those heavy religious associations. In Ancient Near Eastern cosmology the gods were "up." In Hebrew Scripture, Moses receives the Law on a mountain; God comes to Elijah on a mountain. Matthew is subtly making the connection between the Rabbi Jesus, who assumed the authoritative position and sat to teach, and great figures from Israel's past. Then Matthew says "the disciples came to him." Are the disciples different from the crowd? Were they especially called out from it to hear this teaching? Scholars answer the questions in various ways. The point is that Jesus "began to teach"; the verb form in Greek implies that he will continue to do so: this is a beginning.

The Beatitudes that follow served Matthew's community as words of encouragement in their suffering. Matthew's gospel, like Mark's, suggests that to follow Jesus inevitably leads to suffering. Scholars think that Matthew's community is probably in the process of defining itself over and against its roots in the synagogue from which it has been excluded or has departed. The Jewish Christians in Matthew's community are suffering the dislocation of separation from their former religious community that occurred after the Council of Jamnia about 80 to 85 C.E.

The Beatitudes occur in the context of and introduce the subject of Christian, as contrasted with Pharisaic, righteousness (5:1–6:18). Augustine noted that they are "with regard to good morals, the perfect standard of the Christian life."[2] Many scholars regard them as the fundamental laws of the kingdom of God, the theme of which is the righteousness the King requires. While the followers of Jesus will inherit the kingdom, they will also experience earthly distresses like sorrow, hunger, mourning, persecution, and yearning. In the Beatitudes we see both the character and the privileges of the subjects of God's kingdom. Indeed, the Beatitudes are the "marching orders" for that kingdom.

Literary Form

If the Beatitudes are not the actual words of Jesus, they certainly represent his teaching accurately. Both Matthew (5:3-12) and Luke (6:20-23) record a version of them. Source criticism of the New Testament suggests that they come from the Synoptic gospel source we call "Q" (a sayings collection common to Matthew and Luke) and from "M," Matthew's own, special material. Matthew has placed them at the beginning of the first of five discourses Jesus delivers in his gospel. Thus they set the tone for everything that follows.

Beatitudes are expressions of praise or congratulation and thus belong to the literary genre known as ascription. A beatitude or macarism begins with the Greek adjective *makarios* and is followed by a pronoun that introduces the clause explaining the quality or conduct that prompted the blessedness (the *hoti* clauses in the Greek). Usually they are formulated in the third person singular, but that is not universal. In ancient literature there existed both religious macarisms (like Ps 1:1) and secular macarisms that praised people for wealth, strength, wisdom, etc.[3] Beatitudes may bless humans because of their present circumstances, but also for what lies in store for them in the

---

[2] Augustine of Hippo, *Commentary on the Lord's Sermon on the Mount,* ed. Denis J. Kavanagh (New York: Fathers of the Church, Inc., 1951) 19. (Hereafter cited as Kavanagh.)

[3] Hans Dieter Betz, "The Beatitudes of the Sermon on the Mount" in idem, *Essays on the Sermon on the Mount* (Philadelphia: Fortress, 1985) 25.

future.[4] Many scholars think Matt 5:3-12 is of this latter sort, that these are "eschatological blessings," the rewards of God to believers at the denouement of history.

As a literary form beatitudes occur in many ancient literatures, but especially in Greek and Hebrew. There are at least 45 beatitudes in the Hebrew Bible, most of which are found in the wisdom literature and are declarative statements that function as exhortations. The New Testament contains about 37 beatitudes, 17 of which occur in the gospels as sayings of Jesus.[5]

Structure

Matthew's Beatitudes are as follows:

3 Blessed are the poor in spirit, for theirs is the kingdom of heaven.
4 Blessed are those who mourn, for they shall be comforted.
5 Blessed are the meek, for they shall inherit the earth.
6 Blessed are those who hunger and thirst for righteousness, for they shall be satisfied.
7 Blessed are the merciful, for they shall obtain mercy.
8 Blessed are the pure in heart, for they shall see God.
9 Blessed are the peacemakers, for they shall be called children of God.
10 Blessed are those who are persecuted for righteousness' sake, for theirs is the kingdom of heaven.

There is, in fact, discussion about the actual number of Beatitudes in the Sermon on the Mount. Some scholars argue for seven (5:3-9), some eight (viewing vv. 10-12 as one beatitude), and some nine (5:3-12). It is certainly the case that this is not a random list, but a carefully patterned collection. In his 1905 commentary, *The Gospel According to St. Matthew*, A. Carr sug-

---

[4] Dale C. Allison, *The Sermon on the Mount: Inspiring the Moral Imagination* (New York: Crossroad, 1999) 41.
[5] Raymond Collins, "Beatitude," *ABD* 1:629–31.

gests the Beatitudes present a pattern of Christian growth. It begins with the poor in spirit. Spiritual poverty allows one to receive the benefits of repentance. The poor know they need. This spiritual poverty leads to sadness for sin, the "sorrow" or "mourning" of v. 4. The meek (v. 5), those of gentle spirit, are ready to be submissive to God's will. They are like Jesus who is "gentle and lowly in heart" (Matt 11:29) or like the psalmist in Psalm 131 whose "eyes are not raised too high," who is not occupied "with things too great and too marvelous." The meek one hungers and thirsts for righteousness (v. 6), which is manifested by the three virtues of Christian life: mercy (v. 7), purity (v. 8), and peacemaking (v. 9).[6]

Hebrew poetry often exhibits synonymous parallelism in sets of two, three, or four. This has led scholars to divide the Beatitudes into two groups of four lines, two parallel stanzas. In Greek each of these quatrains has 36 words.[7] The first four (vv. 3-6) emphasize the persecuted character of Jesus' disciples and God's reversals on their behalf, and the last four (vv. 7-10) list the ethical qualities that have led to their persecution and the rewards that will be theirs. The righteousness of which the Beatitudes speak refers in vv. 3-6 to divine justice (those who *will* inherit the kingdom) and in vv. 7-10 to their good conduct. Verses 3 and 10 end with "kingdom of heaven," marking off an inclusion. All the groups listed in vv. 3-6 begin in the Greek with "p": poor (*ptochoi*), mourning (*penthountes*), meek (*praeis*), and hungering (*peinontes*). Verses 5 and 9 work on the basis of a family metaphor, the inheritance that comes to children, and thus to heirs. Verses 6 and 10 begin with the idea of righteousness, so the last verse of each "stanza" balances. The first stanza deals with those who have been deprived of the justice of righteousness, and the second speaks of those who are dedicated to its establishment. David Garland has noted that in an arrangement of two stanzas of four beatitudes (vv. 3-6 and vv. 7-10) the

---

[6] A. Carr, *The Gospel According to St. Matthew* (Cambridge: Cambridge University Press, 1905) 55.

[7] Kavanagh, *Reading Matthew,* 365.

first group pertain to one's disposition toward God and the second one's attitude toward others.[8] It is worth remembering that this is roughly the pattern set forth in the Ten Commandments and in the Lord's Prayer as well. In all three teachings relations with God precede relations with others. Church Fathers Polycarp and John Chrysostom both noted that the "poor in spirit" (v. 3) are, in fact, the persecuted of v. 10 so that the Beatitudes form a sort of "golden chain" linking consolation and activity.

To understand the Beatitudes properly, we need to have some sense of the meaning of the terms "blessed" and "kingdom of heaven."

"Blessed"/*Makarios*

Unfortunately in some modern English translations the Greek work *makarioi* is rendered "happy." This doesn't make theological or logical sense. The etymological root of "happy" is *hap* and means "chance," as in "happenstance." But certainly Christian blessedness isn't a matter of chance! We Christians do not live under the rule of the Fates or the goddess Fortuna. Nor does "happy" as a translation make logical sense, as "happy are they who mourn" illustrates. Anybody who has mourned will tell you they were *not* happy! As St. Augustine notes about this beatitude, "mourning is a sorrowful thing, for it is the sob of one who is sorry."[9] The Greek verb *makarizō* means "consider fortunate." It does not mean "happy" in the emotional sense, as modern English uses the word, but suggests success or prosperity as in a formula of congratulation. A makarism was a familiar ascription in the Greek world; it was used to congratulate people who in some way shared the privileged state of the gods.[10] In 1 Timothy 1:11 the word is used in connection with God, "who is worthy of all praise," suggesting a deeply religious connotation for the term.

---

[8] David Garland, *Reading Matthew* (New York: Crossroad, 1993) 54.
[9] Kavanagh, 365.
[10] Garland, *Reading Matthew,* 52–53.

"Blessedness," then, does not describe the feelings or emotional state of those to whom it is applied. The "blessed" might well be miserable! They are assigned the term "blessed" from an ideal point of view. They are to be congratulated for having divine approval. Indeed, in the Greek text of the Beatitudes there is no "to be" verb, no "are." In Greek these are not statements, but exclamations, like those that might begin with the Hebrew *ashere*: "O, the bliss of!" William Barclay called them "congratulations on present bliss."[11] Other scholars have argued that the Beatitudes view things from God's point of view. They are sometimes called "eschatological blessings," God's congratulations, which will find fulfillment in the lives of God's beloved. In this sense "congratulations" is a much better rendering than "happy" for *makarioi*, although I prefer the traditional "blessed."

Kingdom of Heaven

"The Synoptic Gospels contain 76 different kingdom sayings. . . ."[12] The term "kingdom of heaven" occurs 32 times in Matthew's gospel. Matthew prefers the term "heaven" to "God" because he was writing for a Jewish Christian community that would be hesitant to use the name of God. I quote these numbers simply to suggest that "kingdom of God/heaven" is a major, if not *the* major point in the teaching of Jesus. Matthew has indicated in 4:17, 23 and 9:35 (compare 10:7) that the nearness of the kingdom *was* the Gospel, the Good News Jesus proclaimed. It called for repentance, or turning again (4:17) and was attested by miracles (9:35). All of Matthew 13 is devoted to kingdom parables, and it is instructive to read that chapter and then to examine the Beatitudes in its light.

---

[11] William Barclay, *The Beatitudes and the Lord's Prayer for Everyman* (New York: Harper and Row, 1968) 15.

[12] C.C. Caragounis, "Kingdom of God/Heaven" in Joel B. Green, et al., eds., *Dictionary of Jesus and the Gospels* (Downers Grove, IL: InterVarsity Press, 1992) 425.

But what does the phrase mean? "Kingdom of heaven" is shorthand for the reign of God, which Jesus comes to proclaim and inaugurate. Perhaps calling it the "reign" of God rather than the "kingdom" of God makes it clear that we are not speaking about real estate, about land. "Kingdom" signifies "God's . . . sovereign, dynamic and eschatological . . . rule."[13] The idea is in continuity with both Hebrew scriptural and Jewish apocalyptic thinking, but on Jesus' lips it differed from both in that it "denoted God's eternal rule rather than an earthly kingdom, its scope was universal rather than limited to the Jewish nation, and it was imminent and potentially present in him rather than a vague, future hope. . . ."[14] The phrase refers "to the ideal, eschatological state, when, in the words of the Lord's Prayer, God's will 'will be done on earth as it is in heaven.'"[15] The coming of the kingdom had messianic associations for Jesus' hearers, so to speak of the kingdom was to speak of God's rescue and deliverance in historical and political as well as personal terms. In our day anyone who says the followers of Jesus should avoid politics hasn't understood his preaching of the kingdom. "Kingdom" moves us from the personal to the corporate or political and reminds us that Gospel living is always life in and for community.

In Matthew's gospel in particular, the kingdom of heaven idea frames the Beatitudes and also forms the first petition of the Lord's prayer. For Matthew, concern for the kingdom of heaven takes precedence over all other concerns. It is sobering to note that, at the end of the Sermon on the Mount, Jesus says entrance into the kingdom depends not on lip service, but on performance of God's will (Matt 7:21). And so we turn (finally!) to the Beatitudes themselves.

[13] Ibid. 417.
[14] Ibid.
[15] Allison, *Sermon*, 46.

Matthew 5:3: Blessed are the poor in spirit, for theirs is the kingdom of heaven.[16]

It is crucial to understand what the word poor *(ptōchos)* means. It is an adjective describing someone who is completely destitute. Luke chooses it to describe Lazarus in Luke 16:20-21. It is used 38 times in the LXX and refers to those oppressed by the rich and powerful. The "poor" in the Psalms (9:13, 34:10) and elsewhere (Isa 49:13, 61:1) are the class of needy righteous who suffer at the hands of the ungodly, but trust in God. They are tied in the OT to the *ani*, the poor, humble, faithful whose trust is only in God; they are the "first cousins" of the "Remnant." (See Isa 11:4; 29:19; 32:7; 61:1; Amos 2:7; 8:4; Zeph 2:3.) The "poor" are those who could not make a living without working at jobs that made them ritually impure. (See, for example, John 7:49.) They are of special concern throughout the letter of James (which liberally quotes Matthew) as those chosen to be "poor in the world" but "rich in faith and heirs of the kingdom" (Jas 2:5). The "poor" are the *am-ha'aretz,* the quiet in the land, the little people who tried to be religiously observant but were troubled both by economic necessity and religious and political oppression. Scholarship suggests they are probably the group from which Jesus himself came. If Robert Gundry is correct and Isa 61:1-2 is the text behind the Sermon on the Mount, what we have here are the oppressed who cry out for deliverance and rely on God to provide it. As opposed to those who have access to power and visible means of support, the poor depend upon God.

"Poor of spirit" also implies personal inadequacy.[17] So Augustine, says: "the poor in spirit are rightly understood as the humble and the God-fearing . . . those who do not have a bloated spirit."[18] Matthew has taken the social condition of

---

[16] For an extended exposition of this beatitude see Betz, "Beatitudes," 26–33.

[17] Robert Gundry, *Matthew: A Commentary on His Literary and Theological Art* (Grand Rapids: Eerdmans, 1982) 67.

[18] Kavanagh, 21.

Luke's beatitude (Luke 6:20) and spiritualized it. The "poor in spirit" "acknowledge their spiritual need."[19] It is not only the rich who will have trouble entering the kingdom; it is the self-confident, the "actualized," the self-sufficient. Those who are not ill, or who don't know they are sick, *seek* no physician! The inadequate, the broken, the spiritually "afflicted" are close to the kingdom and, in fact, are its citizens. The Greek literally says "heaven rules them."[20] The poor in spirit live in acknowledgment of their impoverishment before God. They know themselves to be the "king's subjects." Jesus says awareness of the need for God makes one more receptive to God's reign.[21] This Beatitude clearly flies in the face of our self-sufficient, self-actualized praising culture. It says, in fact, that those who are aware of their own personal inadequacy, not the strong or "able," are *now* ("theirs *is*" the kingdom: italics mine) in God's reign.

Excursus

It should be noted that the order of 5:4-5 is uncertain. Some ancient manuscripts of Matthew place v. 5 before v. 4, and J. Fenton thinks there are good grounds for thinking that was the original order.[22] I have preserved the commonly accepted order found in the major English translations of the NT.

Matthew 5:4: Blessed are those who mourn, for they shall be comforted.

The word for "mourn," *penthein*, is one of the strongest expressions for mourning in Greek and is usually used for mourning the dead. God has anointed One who will "comfort all who

---

[19] Allison, *Sermon*, 44–45. For an interesting article that makes the startling point that Christianity is a religion for the broken and sick see Donald E. Gowan, "Salvation as Healing," *Ex Auditu* 5 (1989) 1–19.

[20] Mark Allen Powell, "Matthew's Beatitudes: Reversals and Rewards of the Kingdom," *CBQ* 58 (1996) 465.

[21] Garland, *Reading Matthew*, 55.

[22] J. Fenton, *Saint Matthew* (London: Penguin, 1963) 80.

mourn." (See Isa 61:2.) Those mourners may well be lamenting the sins of Israel that thwart God's purposes and delay the kingdom.[23] Or they may be mourning the abject condition of the persecuted disciples.[24] Certainly the cause for mourning must include, but not be limited to, bereavement, mourning for one who has died. Mourning here refers both to personal and private sorrows and to public and social remorse or regret. The Sermon on the Mount always points us toward the social and communal.

William Barclay says "the way to God is the way of the broken heart."[25] (And see Ps 51:17). The point is the promised encouragement or comfort. "Comfort" (*paraklethesontai* in Greek) is a passive compound verb formed from the preposition *para*, near or beside, and the verb *kaleō*, to call. From it comes "paraclete," "comforter" as it is frequently translated in John's gospel, especially in chapters 14 to 16. It means to comfort, console, summon to one's side as a helper. The passive voice is a "divine passive," which indicates that it is God who does the comforting. Again, because of reticence about use of the divine name some writers of the first century used passive voice to indicate God was the actor. In the Jewish tradition "Comforter" is another designation for the Messiah, but in Christianity it also refers to the Holy Spirit, which Jesus promised as a way God continues with God's people. (See John 14–16.) The Revelation to John reports that the dwelling of God will be with people: "God himself will be with them; he will wipe away every tear from their eyes, and death shall be no more, neither shall there be mourning nor crying nor pain any more, for the former things have passed away" (Rev 21:4).

If poverty of spirit reminds people to be conscious of the need for God, mourning is the appropriate response to God's exclusion from public affairs. Those who mourn sympathize with the tragic in life, with those whose circumstances are far from ideal,

---

[23] W. C. Allen, *The Gospel According to St Matthew* (Edinburgh: T & T Clark, 1922) 41.

[24] Gundry, *Matthew*, 68.

[25] Barclay, *Beatitudes*, 33.

with the suffering. Disciples of Jesus mourn because of their own private sorrows, but also because of human disobedience to God and its unhappy results. The disciples are those who sorrow for and are in solidarity with the sin, sadness and suffering of the world. This mourning leads to God's comforting. They shall be comforted when God's kingdom comes and God's will is done.[26] This beatitude calls not for radical separation from the world (which is how religious life has often been envisioned), but for open-heartedness in response to it; it calls us to take the sorrows of the world into our own hearts and then to do something to alleviate them.

Matthew 5:5: Blessed are the meek, for they shall inherit the earth.

In Hebrew "poor" and "meek" are frequently used synonymously. Note the correspondence between Jesus and Moses, who "was very meek, more than all men that were on the face of the earth" (Num 12:3). Moses, the giver of the first law from Mount Sinai, is now followed by another "meek" one, Jesus (Matt 11:29), who is giving the new law from a mountain. Matthew is at pains to paint Jesus as a new Moses. He, too, was endangered by a ruler's slaughtering of male Hebrew children. He, too, went down to Egypt. He, too, is giving Torah from a mountain. The parallels quickly become obvious.[27]

Meekness (which is used as an adjective only here and in Matt 11:29 and 1 Peter 3:4) implies acceptance of the lowly position that "poor" would indicate.[28] Recent scholarship identifies the *praeis* as "the oppressed" or "the powerless."[29] *Praus* in Greek[30] translates the Hebrew word *anaw*, one who accepts whatever

---

[26] Fenton, *Saint Matthew*, 81.

[27] For more on Moses see Allison, *Sermon*, 48.

[28] Gundry, *Matthew*, 69.

[29] Powell, "Matthew's Beatitudes," 466.

[30] For a book-length study of the term see Klaus Wengst, *Humility: Solidarity of the Humiliated* (Philadelphia: Fortress, 1988).

God sends and is thus dear to God. (See the commentary above on "poor.") In the Greek world meekness was a slave virtue to which nobody would aspire. The poor, in material possessions or in spirit, have no right to haughtiness. But they do, according to Christianity, have an inheritance. (See 1 Peter 5:5b-7.) To "inherit the earth" is in addition to the kingdom, which Jesus has said belongs to the poor, thus strengthening the parallel with 5:3. But if the word "meek" implies "the oppressed," then it is noteworthy that they will inherit "earth" or "land." The suggestion is of the reversal of economic oppression. What is implied in these beatitudes has radical social as well as spiritual application.

The choice (and it must be a choice, as our discussion of humility in Chapter Four will insist) of a lowly position is precisely what Jesus' words and example demand of his disciples. Disciples are to be wary of those who take the best places at dinner or in synagogue. The "seen" vs. "in secret" sequence in 6:1-17 may well be the examples, the "object lessons" for this injunction to humility. The Christian way is, in humility, to count others better than ourselves even as Jesus humbled himself and became obedient even to death on a cross. (See Phil 2:1-11 for a powerful exposition of the point.) It is *after* this act of humility that God highly exalted him (Phil 2:3, 8-9). Interestingly, one of the few things Jesus says directly about himself is that he is "meek and humble of heart" (Matt 11:29). As Augustine noted, "the meek are those who do not resist the will of God."[31] We might say the meek are those who pray "thy will be done" and mean it! Moreover, meekness involves acting with gentleness when it is within one's power to be severe and stern; thus it is tied to mercy in 5:7. And it implies that the meek are, in some mysterious way, empowered. This bears pondering.

In the Beatitudes (as in 1 Peter) the exaltation that follows humility is presented in terms of inheritance. The noun *kleronomos*, formed from the verb *kleronomesousin*, means literally "heir," one who receives what is promised. The word is

---

[31] Kavanagh, 364.

so used in Galatians 3 and 4; "if you are Christ's then you are
. . . heirs according to the promise" (Gal 3:29). Galatians 4:1-7
and the relationship there suggested between heirs of the kingdom sheds much light on the nature of the inheritance of the
meek. Those who have not even self-esteem, those who acknowledge complete dependence on God, will receive more than the
apparent "owners" and "rulers" of this world (as, indeed, Mary
seems to have known; see Luke 1:47-55, especially vv. 51-53).
Again, this is a powerfully countercultural promise, and it is
worth recalling that "inherit . . . connotes not a reward that one
must earn but a gift for which one must only wait."[32] Verse 5 is a
strong assertion of what St. Paul calls "the grace of God."

Matthew 5:6: Blessed are those who hunger and thirst for righteousness, for they shall be satisfied.

This is a particularly hard Beatitude for those who have never
been hungry or thirsty to understand. One quickly sees how it is
good news to the poor and humble. "Hunger" and "thirst" are
strong physical needs and suggest the intensity of those seeking
righteousness. They are also easily associated with the poor. The
verb for "satisfied" (*chortasthesontai*) is used in both the LXX
and the New Testament in relationship to feeding, to being filled
or "satisfied" by a good meal.

Here again there are echoes of the prophecies of Isaiah. God
called out prisoners; "they shall not hunger or thirst" (Isa
49:10). "Ho, every one who thirsts, come to the waters; and he
who has no money, come buy and eat" (Isa 55:1). Behind these
verses in Isaiah are the "poor" of v. 3 who will receive God's lib-
erality. Here, as there, the situation is spiritualized, as the hunger
and thirst are for righteousness, for what God requires, but the
metaphor has physical intensity. Longing for God's righteousness and justice is described in physical terms.

---

[32] Powell, "Matthew's Beatitudes," 467.

"Righteousness" (*dikaiosunē*) appears only 10 times in the New Testament, 7 times in Matthew, who appeals to the Hebrew scriptural sense of "true religion" as a life pervaded by God's presence and direction. Interestingly, the blessing is pronounced on unfulfilled aspiration. Intent and aim in life, not achievement, are crucial in Jesus' teaching. (See, for example, Matt 5:21-48 and Jesus' concern for motivation.) Again, this is a highly countercultural idea in the modern West. It is, indeed, a comforting word, if one that has led to theological controversy. The Fathers and Roman Catholic interpreters have tended to assume that "righteousness" refers to behavior according to God's will; what we do that is in God's will. Protestant exegetes see righteousness as *God's* action either in justification or in eschatological justice, which is promised at the last day. Probably the Catholic view is more in accord with that of Matthew. But, as Dale Allison points out, 5:6 does "not congratulate those who are as a matter of fact righteous. Instead it encourages those who are hungering and thirsting for conformity to the will of God."[33]

But both "hunger" and "thirst" are driving words, words with all too little content for most Western Christians. The story is told of a man who came to the Buddha seeking enlightenment. The Buddha held his head under the water of a river, then asked him, "what do you want most?" "Air," the man gasped. The Buddha replied, "when you want enlightenment as much as air, you will receive it." To be satisfied, one must really yearn for righteousness. "Only those whose deepest longings are for fellowship with God will know the comfort that can be supplied only by God."[34] The beatitude says we must long for righteousness as a starving person longs for food. The question is: are we starved for justice? Again it is worth emphasizing that it is not the one who has attained righteousness but the one who hungers for it whom the Beatitudes assert God blesses.

[33] Allison, *Sermon*, 49.
[34] Garland, *Reading Matthew*, 56.

This yearning for righteousness will be manifested in action, in mercy, purity, and peacemaking, the subject of the next three Beatitudes, and it may lead to persecution, the subject of the last. So 5:6 is the "hinge" beatitude. The first four beatitudes "speak of reversal of circumstances for those who are unfortunate."[35] In these beatitudes we learn for whom John the Baptist's and Jesus' announcement of the nearness of the kingdom is good news. God's reign does not sound appealing to those *on* the thrones or to the rich who are promised emptiness, but to the poor, mourning, meek, marginalized, and downtrodden ones. Those "whom Jesus declares blessed in 5:7-10 are those who help to bring to reality the blessings promised to others in 5:3-6."[36] Those who receive mercy, see God, are God's children, are those who look out for the ones who cannot look after themselves, who associate with them and thus become numbered among them.

Matthew 5:7: Blessed are the merciful, for they shall obtain mercy.

"Merciful" is from the Hebrew word *hesed*, which is used 150 times in the OT to describe the action of God, usually in connection with the Covenant. This Greek form of the word "merciful" (*eleēmones*) is found in the New Testament only here and in Heb 2:17, where the Christ is described as "a merciful and faithful high priest in the service of God." Thus to be merciful is to be Christ-like. "Mercy" is active, not emotive. It is "pitiful loving-kindness toward the unfortunate."[37] Luke's parable of the Good Samaritan (Luke 10:29-37) is told to answer the question "who is my neighbor?" The answer is "the one who showed mercy," to which Jesus replies, "go and do likewise." Mercy is manifested in action and has to do with "outgoing love" that is

---

[35] Powell, "Matthew's Beatitudes," 469.

[36] Ibid. 470.

[37] B.T.D. Smith, *The Gospel According to St Matthew* (Cambridge: Cambridge University Press, 1950) 92.

naturally individualized. Here there is no room for "I love humanity, it's people I hate."

The idea of mercy has to do with treating others as one wishes to be treated. This is the "like for like" beatitude, a call for reciprocity. Psalm 18:25-26 states this idea clearly. God is loyal to the loyal, blameless with the blameless, pure with the pure, but harsh to the crooked. Jesus expresses the same idea in the Lord's prayer: "Forgive us our debts as we also have forgiven our debtors" (Matt 6:12, the only petition with an explanation, 6:14-15), in the "Golden Rule," and in the expression "the measure you give will be the measure you get" (Mark 4:24, Luke 6:38). The same idea is behind the discussions of greatness and forgiveness in Matthew 18. To Aristotle, pity was a troublesome emotion that needed dramatic tragedy to exorcize it. To Jesus, pity manifested as mercy was a divine emotion that he expected to be carried out in acts of benevolence, especially for and with the poor and disenfranchised. To show mercy to them was to show mercy to himself. (See Matt 25:31-46.)

In Shakespeare's tragedy, *The Merchant of Venice,* Portia says to Shylock, "in the course of justice, none of us should see salvation." If we receive what we give, we are lost, for mercy requires not only that we do not seek revenge, but that we overcome all attitudes of vindictiveness, jealousy, and littleness. "Mercy requires that we sow good seed in our enemy's field."[38] In this regard our only prayer must be, "God, be merciful to *me,* a sinner" (Luke 18:13, italics mine). The writer of James, who seems to have known Matthew's gospel well, provides the best gloss on mercy. "For judgment is without mercy to one who has shown no mercy; yet mercy triumphs over judgment" (Jas 2:13). Mercy, not justice, is the moral center of Christianity, as the words and actions of Jesus everywhere attest. If we want peace, we must do mercy.

---

[38] Charles Allen, *The Beatitudes: An Interpretation* (Old Tappan, NJ: Fleming H. Revell Co., 1967) 4.

Matthew 5:8: Blessed are the pure in heart, for they shall see God.

Again, the words of the Psalmist focus the beatitude. "Who shall ascend the hill of the Lord? And who shall stand in His holy place? Whoever has clean hands and a pure heart . . . . will receive blessing from the Lord, and vindication from the God of his salvation" (Ps 24:3-5). But the Greek "pure" (*katharos*) does not mean without blemish, but "unmixed," which would be a better English translation. What is called for here is one-mindedness, an undivided heart. The term "pure" is used in the OT for ceremonial purity. For Jesus it was an attitude of the soul, here called the "heart," the center of the person, person at the most profound level, what Thomas Merton called "the true self." The call is to be centered in our deepest, truest selves, to strive for a unified life, personal consistency; it is a call to integrity.

Practically, the sixth Beatitude was good news to the poor who by virtue of their work could not avoid ritual defilement. It indicates that the only thing that can prevent access to God comes from within. (Compare Matt 15:10ff.) To see God is to possess the kingdom, and both are realizable in proportion to purity of heart.[39] First John clarifies the point. "Beloved, we are God's children now; it does not yet appear what we shall be, but we know that when he appears we shall be like him, for we shall see him as he is. And everyone who thus hopes in him purifies himself as he is pure" (1 John 3:2-3). "Seeing" here suggests the "inner eyes" in Eph 1:17-18. It implies not only a physical perception of God, but understanding of the divine nature. Those of undivided heart know something of the inner life of God, which is undivided Love.

The notion of being children of God, which was also implicit in the "inheritance" verb in v. 5, occurs again here. Children, if not abused, are pure in heart in their "present-ness," their moment-to-moment one-pointedness, their ability to be focused in

---

[39] Alan H. McNeile, *Matthew* (London: Macmillan, 1955) 52.

the present moment. The humility and purity of children make them near to the kingdom. Indeed, Matthew records that "to such belongs the kingdom of heaven" (Matt 19:14). Luke adds, "whoever does not receive the kingdom of God like a child shall not enter it" (Luke 18:17). And this is the context of greatness in Matthew 18, to become humble like a little child (18:1-4).

The purity here commended is real purity as opposed to the ceremonial purity of the Pharisees later in chapter 5 (and of the hypocrites in chapter 6), what we might call "exterior piety" or even sanctimoniousness. Again, just as hungering and thirsting for righteousness doesn't necessarily mean being righteous, here being pure doesn't mean being sinless. It speaks of one's aspiration, the solitary or singleness of focus of one's desire. It is also the purity to which James refers in Jas 4:7-8. It is a matter of attitude as well as of action, for it originates in the heart, the seat of the will and of thinking, the biblical center of personhood. Purity of heart, then, refers to the whole personality and calls us to be people without "mixed motives." It is, as the Oxford Annotated Bible notes, "single-mindedness or sincerity, freedom from mixed motives; it is not synonymous with chastity, but includes it."[40] Again, James summarizes the point. "Religion that is pure and undefiled before God is this: to visit orphans and widows in their affliction [that is, to help the poor and disenfranchised] and to keep oneself unstained from the world" (Jas 1:27). And that this purity is "of heart" suggests that it begins as an internal matter (see 5:6 above); it bespeaks the "inwardness of true piety,"[41] which is also taught in Matt 6:1-18.

All this leaves us with the interesting question: what does it mean to "see God"? Remember, in the OT nobody could, or very sensibly usually *wanted*, to "see God." In John 4:24 Jesus says God is spirit, suggesting God doesn't have a body one *could* see. But in Matt 18:10 Jesus says that children's guardian angels see the face of God, and in John 14:9 he declares that those who

---

[40] *The Oxford Annotated Bible*, 1175.
[41] Gundry, *Matthew*, 71.

have seen him *have* seen God. I think what is being gotten at here is the idea of glimpsing the divine reality. "To see" in Scripture is a metaphor for "to understand." The point is that those who are one-minded (focused) are more likely to have a glimpse of the reality of God. Gregory of Nyssa says that seeing God will be returning to our Edenic state. But when we have purity of heart we can perceive God's reflection.[42] Focus helps us to see the Reality within reality. If there is a mystical promise in the beatitudes, this is it: the promise that we can have experience of God now, in this world, in the present moment. And this is because, as Luke's Jesus says, the kingdom of God is "among" or "within" us (Luke 17:21). As we work in and for the kingdom, we receive glimpses of its King.

Matthew 5:9: Blessed are the peacemakers, for they shall be called sons [children] of God.

The Greek word for peace evokes the meaning the Hebrew word *shalom*, which implies perfect welfare, serenity, prosperity, and wholeness. It encompasses the notion of right personal relationships within ourselves, toward others, and toward God. Peacemaking, like mercy and purity, are part of the nature of God. God is perfect peace, in perfect relationship to the divine self and to the whole of creation. The two previous qualities, mercy and single-mindedness, are prerequisites of peacemaking. The term "peacemaker" is not used elsewhere in the NT, but in Greco-Roman literature "it applies to rulers who establish security and socioeconomic welfare."[43] In the OT *shalom* and *mishpat*, peace and justice, are parallel.[44] Peace, then, is a deep commitment to the work of justice and mercy. It reminds us that it is important not to spiritualize the Beatitudes, to take them away from their political reality. Here again, the theme of children and heirs comes to the fore. The NT conditions of "sonship"

---

[42] See Allison, *Sermon*, 53.
[43] Powell, "Matthew's Beatitudes," 473.
[44] Ibid. 474.

or family membership are spelled out in Matt 25:34-40; 2 Cor 6:16-18; Gal 3:26–4:7 and 1 John 3:10. Briefly, they are purity, faith, and righteousness, precisely the qualities commended above.

Because they are God's children, peacemakers share the divine nature. As reconcilers, they are also Christ-like, for Christ's mission was to reconcile people to God. This is a mission of more than public significance. It suggests not only external, political work, but making peace within the self and between others. It is both "inter" and "intra." By means of meekness, righteousness, mercy, purity people still their own warring natures and bring peace to themselves and others. Augustine says, "if you would be a peacemaker between two of your friends who are at odds, begin by making peace with yourself. You must first have peace within yourself."[45] A tall order!

But this peace is not simply absence of strife. Elsewhere Jesus says, "I came not to bring peace but a sword" (Matt 10:34). The peace Jesus gives is "not as the world gives" (John 14:27). God's peace "passes all understanding," but "keeps the heart and mind in Jesus" (Phil 4:7). When the will and intellect are "in Jesus," subsumed by his life, in submission to his will, there is peace, no matter what else is going on. In a world that ignores God, to act in accordance with the will of God inevitably leads one into conflict, but in doing God's will one receives the supernatural gift of spiritual peace.

James lifts up the spiritual implications of peacemaking. For James, the wise and understanding are the peaceful (Jas 3:13-18). Heavenly wisdom is pure, peaceful, gentle, merciful, in short, a catalogue of the spiritual qualities mentioned in Matt 5:1-8. Those who make peace reap a great reward. "The harvest of righteousness is sown in peace by those who make peace" (Jas 3:18). And since spiritual peace is inseparable from practical acts of righteousness, we are led to the final Beatitude, which speaks to the persecution that seems to accompany righteous action. It is both a warning and a promise.

[45] Kavanagh, 367.

Matthew 5:10: Blessed are those who are persecuted for righteousness' sake, for theirs is the kingdom of heaven.

In my reading, v. 10 is the beatitude and vv. 11-12 amplify it. Those who hunger and thirst for righteousness and pursue it by mercy, purity, and peacemaking will be misunderstood and persecuted by the world, just as the motives and message of the prophets, of John the Baptist, and of Jesus were misunderstood. This unit of material, 5:10-12, bespeaks the inevitability of persecution for those who seek seriously to follow Jesus. The word "persecuted" (*dediogmenoi)* is from the verb *diokō*, which can also be translated "seek after," "strive for," or "follow" (see v. 6). It implies both physical and verbal abuse. The word underlines that the cause of suffering ("for righteousness sake") is crucial.[46] This is not a call for martyrdom, but an acknowledgment of what can (and does) happen to those who follow Jesus. There is no need to seek suffering in the mode of the old penances or "taking the discipline." It comes "naturally" as a result of one-mindedly living the Christ-like life. Indeed, it is a by-product of it, and a divine promise: "in this world you will have trouble" (John 16:33).

In terms of Matthew's community, those suffering for following Jesus, the tense of the verb suggests that the persecution has already begun. We do not know if it came from the synagogue from which the church had parted or from Roman authorities. That persecution existed is not in doubt. If, as some scholars think, the sermon was directed to leaders of the Christian community (those disciples called out from the crowd in 5:1),[47] then for them persecution is both a test and a token of true discipleship. Verses 11-12 are probably later additions, explanations of the "hard saying" in v. 9 given directly to the disciples. ("Blessed are you" rather than "blessed are they.") They may reflect situations like the one in 1 Peter 4:12-19 in which ordeals are not so much surprises, as opportunities to share Christ's suffering. Re-

---

[46] Carr, *Matthew,* 56.
[47] Smith, *Gospel,* 93–94.

proached for his name, "you are blessed because the spirit of glory and of God rests upon you" (1 Pet 4:14).

Accurate historical reconstruction of Matthew's community is not necessary for understanding these verses. Jesus' program of life would be in conflict with pagan, worldly, materialistic living as well as with synagogue practice as Matthew seems to have understood it. The graces of the Beatitudes have always been impractical and dangerous, but they end with a note of both warning and consolation. Righteousness leads to persecution. It also leads to the kingdom. We have come full circle to those who are persecuted for the sake of doing justice to and with the poor. The poor and the persecuted are the same people, the citizens of the kingdom of heaven, the heirs of God, and siblings to each other.

Conclusion

The following long quotation from Charles Allen's book on the Beatitudes accurately summarizes the practical meaning of the Beatitudes for us:

> To be poor in spirit means to give up our pride; to mourn means to be penitent to the point of surrendering our sins; meekness means that we must surrender our very selves to the plans and purposes of God; our hunger for God means turning away from our ambitions for all things else; to be merciful means to pay good for the evil we have received; for purity we must give up all things impure; to make peace is wholly to choose God. Those are the seven ingredients of righteousness. They must be bought at a price. Blessed are those who pay the price, "for theirs is the kingdom of God."[48]

In closing it is important to note that the kingdom of heaven, which the Beatitudes proclaim, is not just a future promise but a present reality, an immediate possibility, an experience limited only by our capacity to desire it and live toward it. In my mind

---

[48] Allen, *Beatitudes*, 60–61.

Jesus' Beatitudes and his Mother's Magnificat go together. Mary's soul rejoices because God *is* holy. God's mercy *is* on those who fear God. God *has* shown strength, scattered the proud, put down the mighty, exalted the humble, filled the hungry. The Beatitudes both promise and give the kingdom to the dispossessed, the poor, the hungry, the mourning, in short, to the entire range of the needy.[49] The kingdom of heaven *is*. Blessed *are*. No one who has heard these words is free of their imperative. And for those who hear and follow, the kingdom is already among.

This means that, finally, the Gospel value the Beatitudes hold up for us is hope. It reminds us, in the words of Mark Allen Powell, "that God's rule sets things right for all oppressed people."[50] God blesses the very ones the world would consider least blessed! The more we engage ourselves on their behalf, the more we are merciful, focused, peacemakers, the more likely we are to be persecuted, to find ourselves numbered among the poor in spirit, the mourning, the meek, those who have a physical yearning for righteousness that is God's will. "Those who practice the virtues described in the second stanza may on that account come to be numbered among those described in the first stanza on whose behalf these virtues are exercised."[51] This is God's great joke. I hope you are startled by it.

Dale Allison points out that "the beatitudes were intended to startle."[52] We have heard the Beatitudes so frequently that we sometimes miss their astonishing reversals. Common sense would suggest that the rich, not the poor, are blessed, that the happy, not the mourning, are blessed, that the powerful, not the meek, are blessed. You get the idea. "So the beatitudes have things backward. To take them seriously is to call into question our ordinary values."[53] In a world whose values are a mess, this, to me at least, is good news.

---

[49] Collins, "Beatitudes," 630.
[50] Powell, "Matthew's Beatitudes," 476.
[51] Ibid. 475–76.
[52] Allison, *Sermon*, 43.
[53] Ibid.

Questions for Discussion or Further Thought

1. Appendix One collects several "updated" versions of the Beatitudes. You might find it a helpful exercise to write your own beatitudes. (When I asked one of the communities of the Daughters of Wisdom in the United Kingdom to do this, one saintly ninety-plus-year-old sister immediately called out: "Blessed are they who mind their own business.")

2. Are you or is your community (or parish or family) "hungering and thirsting" for justice, or are you in the "circle up the wagons" mode? Are you opening up for justice or closing down to protect what you have? What is the relationship between justice and survival?

3. What would it mean for you to "see God"?

4. What, in practical terms, does it mean to me/to us to be a citizen/citizens of the kingdom of heaven today, right now?

• 2 •

The Kingdom Calls for Charity

Matt 5:13-16, 27-30, 43-48

The next three chapters will highlight the aspect of spiritual maturity that particular vows in religious life were intended to nurture, the spiritual goal toward which they orient us, the kingdom or Gospel value they lift up. We shall be looking at charity, detachment, and humility as the countercultural attitudes to which the Gospel of Jesus Christ calls us, and we shall look at each one in terms of texts from the Sermon on the Mount.

We begin with the old vow of chastity because, in its best *incarnation* (and I use the word intentionally!), it is an invitation to conduct the whole of our life to reflect Gospel values, the most important of which, according to our Lord, is charity or love. When asked by the scribe in Jerusalem "which commandment is the first of all?" Jesus responded by quoting the *Shema,* the great confession of Israel, "you shall love the Lord your God with all your heart, and with all your soul, and with all your mind, and with all your strength. . . . You shall love your neighbor as yourself. There is no other commandment greater than these" (Mark 12:28-31).

The great call to all Christian people is to be lovers. I am using the term "charity" instead of "love" for a reason. Our English language is quite impoverished when it comes to expressing love. "God is love," and "I love chips and beer," and "she loves her husband" all use the same word to express very different things. For most people "love" is an affective word, about emotional life rather than about volition or will, the choice to act in a certain way. The word "charity" in its etymology carries two very useful trajectories of meaning: the Latin *caritas* or love and the Greek *charis* or grace, with all the theology that entails. Charity is benevolent good will toward all humanity especially as it is manifested in active helpfulness to the marginalized, needy, and suffering. It is in this sense that the vow of chastity is a call to charity. It asks of us openheartedness toward everyone instead of toward one special someone. The call to charity is a call to live out the Beatitudes. We are not speaking of charity in the sense of "a charity case," the sense of "doing to" someone we might well look down on. Charity in our sense is to be understood in terms of the selfgiving love of Jesus, which is inclusive in its scope.

Before we turn to the Sermon on the Mount, let us be clear that chastity is not, in its spiritual sense, about virginity or physical intactness. Celibacy, the abstinence from intercourse, and chastity understood as sexual purity (which was often sexual ignorance, what in an essay on celibacy and religious women Kathleen Norris called "criminal naïveté"[1]) is not finally about what we do with the body. Such a limited understanding goes back to a time when human sexuality was neither understood biologically nor considered with healthy openness. To insist that chastity is essentially about genital sexuality is to return us to an age when the sexual drive was feared, when men's fear of their own sexuality led them to fear the very mysterious business of women's sexuality and, in fact, to legislate to control it. There is a very real sense in which the church's obsession with virginity reflects a masculine fear of female generativity and a resultant attempt to control female sexuality. These are not the issues to which we shall address ourselves, although they are important ones to understand.

---

[1] Kathleen Norris, *The Cloister Walk* (New York: Riverhead Books, 1996) 258.

When it comes to revisioning Gospel living, to think of chastity in terms of sexual behavior alone is a dead end. Chastity is for charity's sake. It is *for* life and freedom, not against sexuality. It is a gift to be accepted (and it is gift; not everyone has the gift of chastity) only so that we can be *better* and more inclusive lovers. In her book on the Rule of Benedict, Esther de Waal notes that chastity "taken in its widest sense" means "the refusal to use another person as an instrument for my own pleasure or self-gratification."[2] As Socrates Scholasticus wrote in his *Church History* (1.11), "Intercourse of a man with his lawful wife *is* chastity."[3] (Italics mine.) Furthermore, the acceptance of celibacy does not preclude intimate human relationships; "it makes them more free and open simply because it does not equate loving with sex."[4] Augustine spoke of chastity as "well ordered love" which "does not subordinate greater things to lesser ones."[5] The call to charity, which is the real purpose of celibacy and chastity, is a call to give ourselves as fully as we can, "fully" in the sense of a total gift of person and "fully" in the sense of "as widely as possible," without exclusion. The call of charity is a call to radical availability to others.

With this as our framework, let us look at passages in the Sermon on the Mount that point us toward charity, in particular 5:13-16, 27-30, and 43-48. The general subject of Matthew 5 is interpretation of the Law or Torah. The Beatitudes (5:3-12) paint a new picture of who is (or will be) blessed, of whom God approves. Images of the smallness of those who will accept this new Way are woven together with images of the enormity of their task (5:13-16). Matthew 5:17-48 is often referred to as the "antitheses" because of the literary structure of each unit: "you

---

[2] Esther de Waal, *Seeking God The Way of St. Benedict* (Collegeville: Liturgical Press, 1984) 122.

[3] Quoted in Dale C. Allison, *The Sermon on the Mount* (New York: Crossroad, 1999) 74.

[4] de Waal, *Seeking God,* 124.

[5] Quoted in Enzo Bianchi, *Word of Spirituality* (London, S.P.C.K., 2002) 76.

have heard/but I say to you." In each instance Jesus states the Law, reaffirms it and then radicalizes what, in a real application, it means. Jesus states the principle of his interpretation of the Law in 5:17-20: the Law is not nullified but intensified. He then gives six specific examples. The followers of Jesus are called to be more righteous than the most righteous people of the time, the scribes and Pharisees (5:20). This call is exemplified in matters of interpersonal relationship: anger (5:21-26), marriage (5:27-32), oaths (5:33-37), and revenge (5:21-26). The chapter closes by reminding us that love for the other (charity) summarizes the Law (5:43-47), and that perfection is Jesus' expectation of His followers (5:48). Obviously, this needs some unpacking.

5:13-16

Having made clear who will be blessed in the kingdom of heaven, Jesus turns to these very people and, in poetic form, explains to them what their task will be. As David Garland has noted, "the images of salt, light, and a city on a hill clarify the disciples' vocation in the world."[6] The "you" in Greek is both plural and emphatic, "you, yourselves" as opposed to somebody else or some other group. Jesus is, to put it crudely, "in the face" of his hearers. The Gospel life is imaged by Jesus as a life in community and a life charged with a mission for others. As M. Eugene Boring has written, "like their master, Jesus' disciples live their lives for the sake of the world that persecutes them."[7] We might say they live charity for charity.

In our world the general rule seems to be "bigger is better." We are tempted to buy a box of soap flakes if we get 15% more free. Nobody sells a packet of crackers with the advertisement "30% fewer crackers per box." But in the world of the Spirit, bigger isn't always better; less is sometimes more, and a little is

[6] David Garland, *Reading Matthew* (New York: Crossroad, 1993) 59.
[7] M. Eugene Boring, "Matthew" in Leander E. Keck, et. al., eds., *The New Interpreter's Bible* (Nashville: Abingdon, 1995) 8:181.

sometimes enough. Jesus seems to think a very little is plenty, as the metaphors of salt and light suggest.

Salt was a crucial and highly taxed commodity in Jesus' day. Jews used it in sacrifice as a reminder of the covenant with God. Leviticus records: "You shall not omit from your grain offerings the salt of the covenant with your God; with all your offerings you shall offer salt" (2:13). Salt was necessary for spiritual practice and for physical life; it was the stuff of life, the vital mineral needed to sustain life in a desert world. It was used for purification, for a preservative, as a medicine, as well as for seasoning. Eating together was referred to as "sharing salt." But with salt more isn't better. How much salt would you like in your soup, a pinch or a pound? A little is enough; a lot would spoil the dish.

Disciples are called to be salt in the world, the force for the kingdom that purifies the whole, preserves the creation, gives savor. Jesus knew there would not be many true disciples, many who lived the Gospel way, but the small number that do so makes all the difference. (See, for examples, the parables on this matter in Mark 4.) This is why it is important that we not "lose our saltiness" or become insipid. In Jesus' day salt could be mixed with other elements, and then it was "good for nothing." If we Gospel people, few though we are, are to salt the world, it is important that we not lose our saltiness by becoming mixed, too much like the world in which we live. The Gospel life Jesus envisions is radically different from "the world" in which he calls us to live it, and for whose sake we live it.

The image of light is similar. In a world without light, a little goes a long way. No electricity. No gas lights. No kerosene. Not even candles. For most people in Jesus' day, light was a bit of rag in a bowl of oil. It was dark, smoky light, but on a dark night how bright it must have seemed, what comfort it must have given! Disciples are to be lights in the world. Even our small, smoky light is a beacon that can help others see things as they are, for that is what light does. Our light is to shine before others; indeed, it can not be hidden. "The primary function of light is not to be seen, but to let things be seen as they are. In a provocative contrast, the metaphor of the city on a hill presents the disciples as inevitable and unavoidably *being* seen. . . ."[8] We "enlightened" people are like cities on hills. When we shine with the light of Christ we can't help but illuminate others. When we do not let the Lord's light shine through us, we deepen the darkness.

In Jesus' day cities were built on hills because they were easier to defend, but they could also be seen from far away. Jerusalem was a city on a hill. In Matt 5:14 "the city set on a mountain is a transparent metaphor for Jerusalem. . . ."[9] Isaiah understood that one day all the nations would stream to it to learn God's ways and live in the peace of God (Isa 2:2-5). If disciples are like cities on hills they are, indeed, "lights to the nations" (Isa 42:6; 49:6).

Why are we called to be salt and light? Just for the joy of being salty? Come on! How many of us would eat salt alone? Are we light for the pleasure of bringing attention to ourselves, of being "in the spotlight," as it were? Most of us would rather cower in the wings than be out on the stage! No, we are to be salt and light so that others may "taste and see that the Lord is good," (Ps 34:8) so that others may see what we do and give glory to the God who makes us who we are. There may not be many of us. Salt and light were in short supply in Jesus' day, and he knew it. But Jesus seems to think that what there is will be enough for his purposes. Our saltiness and our light will give glory to God, will preserve and heal and flavor God's world, will light people on God's way to God's city. God calls us so that we can bless others.

"You are the salt of the earth." "You are the light of the world." These are wonderful messages for *small* groups of *real* disciples. We sometimes think that because we are not many, we are not important or potent. But that is not the message of these verses. Bigger isn't always better. A small amount is sometimes enough. It is important, I think, for men and women religious, and Christian people generally, to focus not on diminishment, but on saltiness. Indeed, as we *are* diminished we become those

8 Ibid. 182.
9 Garland, *Reading Matthew*, 59.

whom the Beatitudes say are divinely blessed. "With these three metaphors of salt, light, and city, the Matthean Jesus strikes the death blow to all religion that is purely personal and private."[10] Our personal commitment to charity is for a very public transformation that God intends to effect through us.

5:27-30

I want to focus this chapter on the transition from the Beatitudes (5:13-16) and the closing paragraphs of the anthesis section of the Sermon on the Mount (5:43-48). But I want to pause at 5:27-30 because it has to do with, well . . . sex! Adultery is a case in point of anti-charity. You know this, so I won't belabor it. Jesus' sharpening of the 7th commandment concerning adultery is presented in terms of the 10th commandment not to covet, the prohibition against desire for what is not one's own.[11] Unfortunately, like the 10th commandment in Exod 20:17, it views the wife as a piece of property; adultery deprives a man of what is rightfully his. Without going into the technicalities of ancient property rights or the common view of women as temptresses to sexual sin, we might note that the thrust of the teaching is against predatory behavior of males against females, curbs male power in a patriarchal society, and suggests the possibility for a very different way for men and women to relate.[12] As Douglas Hare suggests, "in Jesus' ministry and in the subsequent fellowship of the church . . . women were not avoided as seductresses but welcomed as sisters. . . . The new relationship with women among Jesus' followers required of men a new kind of self-discipline."[13]

To "covet the neighbor's wife" is to sin against charity in the terms we have been thinking about here. The Hebrew verb for

[10] Boring, "Matthew," 182.

[11] David Hill, *The Gospel of Matthew* (Grand Rapids: Eerdmans, 1984) 123.

[12] See the note on 5:27-30 in *The New Interpreters Study Bible*, 1755.

[13] Douglas R.A. Hare, *Matthew*. Interpretation (Louisville: John Knox, 1993) 53.

covet "implies intentional planning to obtain something for one-self."[14] In contradistinction to detachment (which we shall consider later), one "lusts after" or "grasps for." Lust is a particularly selfish motivation. In contradistinction to being open to love and honor all, the "luster" focuses on one object, "closes down" on self and other. Adultery and lust are a closing down of love that, as Jesus teaches, is meant to be a radical opening up of the person. Adultery and lust as they are presented here refuse to see the person as person, and rather sees "an object for self-gratification."[15] Lust is the ultimate sin against charity because it makes a person a thing. Chastity, or what we have been calling charity, on the other hand is the "refusal to possess, to manipulate, to exploit."[16]

Certainly this sexual morality is conventional. But Jesus radicalizes it by assuming that "God judges not only our deeds but also our thoughts, our intentions."[17] "Matt 5:27-30 is really about controlling the imagination—not about the eyes so much as the soul that uses them."[18] It is not only our actions that must be loving, it is our thoughts and desires as well. When we are chaste in the charitable sense we cannot be selfish on any level of our lives, certainly not in our thoughts about others. Jesus makes it clear that human beings are not to be the passive victims of their natural, normal desires. We have the ability, and indeed the mandate, to direct our sexual lives and, in fact, the whole of the inner life, our thoughts and desires and motivations as well as our actions. Whether vv. 29 and 30 are hyperbolic or to be taken literally, they suggest the seriousness of desire itself, and of its objects. Little wonder Jesus will say in 6:32 "strive first for the kingdom of God and his righteousness!"

---

[14] Ibid. 53.
[15] Garland, *Reading Matthew*, 67.
[16] de Waal, *Seeking God*, 102.
[17] Allison, *Sermon*, 73.
[18] Ibid. 74.

5:43-48

This section on the Law in Matthew closes with the most important and difficult of the commands, first, "love your enemy," and second, "be perfect." We are called to this radical love and to perfection because we are children of God. Verses 45 and 48 each give as the motivation for the action commanded the nature of God, who loves and blesses everyone and who is perfection. (And recall God's nature was highlighted in the Beatitudes, 5:7-9.)

And here is where I am tempted to "check out." How am I to love like this? How am I to be perfect? In fact, I don't *want* to be perfect. I have had troubles enough with people who are perfectionists, and I have given plenty of trouble when I have tried to be one. Perfectionism, we think, is a sort of psychological illness with compulsive behavior as its first cousin and nasty niceness as its great aunt. Does it even makes sense to try to be perfect? Won't that aspiration make me (and everyone who has to deal with me) miserable? When we look at Jesus' commands here I think it is important to understand two things, first the etymology of the Greek word for "perfect" in v. 48, and second its context in the passage.

The Greek word "perfect" *(teleiōi)* is close to a Hebrew word meaning "without spot" or "without moral blemish."[19] In the LXX it was used in relation to men like Noah, "a righteous man, *blameless* in his generation" (Gen 6:9). Matthew's Jesus, however, seems to suggest something more than moral perfection. He suggests the "wholeness and single mindedness by which God goes about fulfilling purposes. . . ."[20] "Perfect" in this sense means "complete, whole, full-grown, mature, accomplished." Disciples are "perfect" when they have "grown up" into Christ. "Perfect" is a particularly important word in Matthew. It is found in the Synoptic Gospels only in Matthew,

---

[19] For a fuller discussion of the term see Bonnie Thurston, "Matthew 5:43-48," *Interpretation* XLI/2 (1987) 170–73.

[20] Key, Young, et.al., *Understanding the New Testament* (Englewood Cliffs, NJ: Prentice Hall, 1965) 284.

and in Matthew three times, each as an insertion in parallel materials. The word occurs in the story of the rich young man (19:16-30) who comes to Jesus saying he has observed all the commandments. Jesus says "if you would be *perfect*, go sell all you possess and give to the poor, and you will have treasure in heaven; and come, follow me" (19:21). As in 5:48, "perfect" occurs in the context of the Law and intensifies it. Matthew's Jesus intensifies the demands of the story to stress the special quality that marks his followers: their perfection is their discipleship, the extent to which they follow him.

Both 5:48 and 19:21 occur with the command to love enemies, an extension of Torah, for, historically, Jews tended to view their compatriots as their neighbors. Enemies were in a whole different moral category. Matthew's Jesus constantly extends who the neighbor is.[21] Perfection in love sees every person from the perspective of God, who sees impartially, making the sun rise on the evil and the good, sending rain on the just and unjust."[22] In both contexts Jesus calls for observable dedication to certain qualities of conduct. Perfection does "not imply complete sinlessness and full virtue as matters of fact."[23] It implies wholeness of consecration to God and acting on that aspiration. So it mirrors the meaning of "pure" ("unmixed") in 5:8. "Perfection," for Matthew's Jesus, is not the condition of having arrived at some state of being; perfection has to do with discipleship—those who are honestly trying to follow Jesus. (An interesting parallel idea is found in Phil 3:2-14, especially vv. 12-14.)

In Matthew's gospel the context of perfection is intensification of Law and discipleship. The love commandment forms the basis of its tradition. It addresses those who have been called to follow Jesus, who was in every way as we are, but without sin,

---

[21] Charles R. Erdman, *The Gospel of Matthew* (Philadelphia: Westminster, 1920) 53.

[22] Willoughby C. Allen, *A Critical and Exegetical Commentary on the Gospel According to St Matthew* (Edinburgh: T & T Clark, 1922) 56.

[23] Robert Gundry, *Matthew: A Commentary on His Literary and Theological Art* (Grand Rapids: Eerdmans, 1982) 388.

blameless before God, Jesus who most perfectly shows God's original intention for all people. Here is perfection in love: Jesus shows us how to be "perfect before the Lord your God" (Deut 18:13). As Gerhard Barth has said, "Following Christ and radical fulfillment of the law are the same."[24] "Pefection" implies wholeness of consecration to God. You can see, I hope, the connection to charity. Perfection is wholehearted discipleship, the desire to follow Jesus and to love as he loved.

Now let us come back to the context in 5:43-48. The "higher standard" is called for in terms of refusal to engage in vengeance, of practicing generosity, and in the struggle against narrow personal preferences in our relationships. Verses 38-41 have made it clear that the *lex talionis* ("eye for eye, tooth for tooth"), must be set aside by disciples of Jesus. They must be willing to allow themselves to be ill treated and not retaliate. They must be more generous than others and give to people who are not "good credit risks." Jesus' disciples are to respond to others in terms of *their* good and *their* needs, not in terms of self interest. The "love command" of 5:43 occurs in this context and is the climax of this section of the Sermon on the Mount. And the context makes clear that the object of love is much broader than most of us would like to imagine. It includes enemies and those who actively persecute us, those persecutors mentioned at the end of the Beatitudes in 5:11-12.

It is easy to love the people we love, to respond to those for whom we have a natural affinity. It is not so easy to love people we would naturally shy away from, or people who repel us. But it is precisely impartiality in loving that is the Gospel value here called for. To be perfect, in short, is to aspire to love as God loves. We are to love our enemies and pray for those who persecute us so that we may be children of God. Children should show a family resemblance to their father and/or mother. (Recall the inheritance/family metaphors of 5:5, 9.) God gives everyone the things that are necessary for life: sun and rain. God doesn't just let the sun rise on

---

[24] Gerhard Barth, "Matthew's Understanding of the Law," in Günther Bornkamm, Gerhard Barth, Held, *Tradition and Interpretation in Matthew* (Philadelphia: Westminster, 1963) 97.

good people and leave evil ones in darkness. God doesn't withhold rain from the unjust and only water the just. God's providential care extends to everybody. God's love is impartial. God loves people whether they are deserving of that love or not.

This, I think, is the perfection that is asked of us. In the verses preceding 5:48 God has been described as impartially caring for all kinds of people. Jesus has pointed out that it is "no big deal" to love our friends and brethren; even tax collectors—the worst sorts of people, turncoats and collaborators with the hated Romans—do that. To be perfect as God is perfect is a call to love as God loves, impartially, universally, selflessly, without restraint or limit or conditions. And this, it seems to me, is precisely what the old vow of celibacy, what we are calling charity, calls us to. Matthew 5:27-30 asks us to purify our loving. Matthew 5:43-48 asks us to perfect it. The degree to which we do so is the degree to which we will be the salt and light spoken of in 5:13-16.

The Kingdom Calls for Charity

In closing, let us go back and think practically about what charity of this sort might mean to us in our day-to-day living. First, charity as we are speaking of it does not preclude "warm relationships, rather it makes them more free and open simply because it does not equate loving with sex."[25] As Kathleen Norris has written, when properly undertaken it has "the potential to address the sexual idolatry of our culture in a most helpful way."[26] The call to charity is not a call to being cold or a-sexual. Indeed, we learn to use the heat of sexual love in a way that will warm others without burning them or ourselves. Real love allows us to be genuinely hospitable to others, to listen to them, to receive all people as the precious, beloved persons they are. In our world very few people experience this sort of love. Charity can be manifested outwardly in hospitality and inwardly in our attitude of availability and openness to others.

[25] de Waal, *Seeking God,* 124.
[26] Norris, *The Cloister Walk,* 116.

For me, charity is a practical call to love especially those the world calls "unlovely," to receive them with special care and tenderness. Catherine of Sienna, that great lover, was asked what it is that we can give God. She responded that the only thing we can give God that would have any value to God is to love others who are as unworthy of our love as we are of God's love. As one woman religious said, the fruit of celibacy is hospitality.[27] Or, as Br. David Steindl-Rast, O.S.B., has written, "Wisdom proves its genuineness through compassion."[28] And of course, "compassion" means "feeling with." According to Brother David, "celibacy is the daring attempt to sustain the 'condition of extreme simplicity' in which solitude and togetherness merge so that aloneness becomes all-oneness."[29]

Second, the great call of Christian charity is a call to freedom both for ourselves and for others. When we seek the perfection of love we are liberated from obsessive behavior in our relationships, and we can, by our example, liberate others. The call to love as God loves is a call to love openly and universally. It frees me from an unhealthy focus on one "object." (I will address this issue in the context of married love in the final chapter.) For this is the great danger of sexual love; it is by its nature exclusive. If I love only one, he or she can become the "*object* of my affection," not a living and growing and radically free *person*. Baron von Hügel, Evelyn Underhill's spiritual director, "once said: 'The best thing we can do for those we love is to help them to escape from us.'"[30] Real love allows the beloved ones their freedom. Esther de Waal points out the paradox of this way of loving when she says: "we enjoy because we do not own; we possess because we renounce possession."[31] We enjoy those we

---

[27] Quoted in ibid., 263.

[28] David Steindl Rast, O.S.B., *A Listening Heart* (New York: Crossroad, 1983/1999) 72.

[29] Ibid. 105.

[30] Quoted in Esther de Waal, *Living with Contradiction: An Introduction to Benedictine Spirituality* (Harrisburg: Morehouse, 1998) 67.

[31] Ibid. 69.

love, and our most profound enjoyment comes from the open-handedness and open-heartedness of our love for them. It is our joy to set them free.

Really loving another is disinterestedly to will and work for the other's good with no particular attention paid to ourselves. And this is the deep, spiritual call of charity. Writing of the Cistercian tradition, Esther de Waal says: "To be open to the good of all was also a sign of being open to God: having nothing of one's own is to need others, and more than that, to need God."[32] Christian charity acknowledges our own need as well as that of others. And it would seem to me to imply charity toward myself, appropriate attendance to my own legitimate needs. We are not different from others; we are profoundly alike. We understand that the deepest of our needs is for God. We will not find the answer to our deepest loneliness in any other human being, but in God alone. Speaking to Kathleen Norris of celibacy, a Benedictine sister said: "One needs a deep prayer life to maintain a celibate life . . . only prayer . . . can give me the self-transcendence that celibacy requires."[33] Perhaps the greatest gift of charity is its potential for opening our hearts more fully to God. Indeed, the challenge of love is the challenge of the completely open heart.

It is so easy to close down heart life, the core of who we are. We feel lonely or misunderstood or wounded or insulted, and we "close up" like turtles pulling ourselves back into our shells. After a few experiences like this, a few woundings, many people close down altogether, become emotionally frigid and die long before they stop breathing. The call of charity is the call fully to live as long as we are alive. Brother David reminds us that we grow in the measure in which we expose our hearts to life, "unshielded, vulnerable, but fully alive."[34] The call of charity is the call to keep the heart fully alive, for only if our hearts are alive will we be deeply connected with God. Charity calls us to have

---

[32] Esther de Waal, *The Way of Simplicity: The Cistercian Tradition* (Maryknoll, NY: Orbis, 1998) 119.

[33] Norris, *The Cloister Walk*, 261.

[34] Steindl-Rast, *A Listening Heart*, 33.

"listening hearts." "A listening heart recognizes in the throbbing of reality pulsating against all our senses the heartbeat of divine life at the core of all that is real."[35]

In her book *The Way of Simplicity: The Cistercian Tradition*, Esther de Waal includes the following passage of St. Aelred. It is a wonderful summary, and a challenge to us.

> That a person may love himself,
> the love of God is formed in him;
> that one may love one's neighbour,
> the capacity of one's heart is enlarged.
> Then as this divine fire grows warmer
> little by little
> it wondrously absorbs the other loves into its fullness,
> like so many sparks.
> And so it leads all the soul's love with it
> to that supreme and ineffable good
> where neither self nor neighbour is loved for self or for neighbour
> but only insofar as each fades away from self
> and is borne totally into God.
> Meanwhile, these three loves
> are engendered by one another,
> nourished by one another,
> and fanned into flame by one another.
> Then they are all brought to perfection together.[36]

Questions for Discussion or Further Thought

1. What are my/our struggles with being fully, openly charitable/loving?

2. In what ways is "less more" for me/us?

3. How can religious, with our decreasing numbers, be salt and light?

4. What are my own continuing struggles with sexuality? Am I still open to them, and thus to myself and to life?

---

[35] Ibid. 45.

[36] Quoted in de Waal, *The Way of Simplicity,* 147.

• 3 •

The Kingdom Calls for Detachment

Matt 6:19-34

We are thinking about the aspect of spiritual maturity that particular vows in religious life were intended to nurture: not the vows, but the end toward which they pointed. Understood in this way, the vows have implications for all Christians. We considered the idea that chastity was intended to develop charity/love. We now continue our reconsideration with poverty, traditionally understood as the call to renounce personal property. In our world and in the Western capitalist economic system that is already a wildly countercultural value. Half the people in the world live to accumulate personal property, to own stuff. The remainder suffer because they do not have the basic necessities. Whether we like it or not, Western economy rests on the idea that the goal is to get richer and richer, to collect more and more things, rather than that the system should evolve in such a way that everyone would have access to life's basic necessities.

Let us be honest and admit, as well, that by the standards of the Two-Thirds' World, religious, and Christians in general, in America and Europe are not poor. Many religious are managing large stock portfolios from the sale of hospitals and schools they once staffed. In general (although there are exceptions that prove the rule), we are well clothed, safely housed, overfed. Indeed, in the United States, even in these years of numerical decline, religious are rich in being able to assume two things most ordinary people can no longer take for granted: access to adequate health care and assurance of loving care in old age. I confess some envy when I see elderly sisters lovingly attended to, often by friends who have known them all their lives. Few of us in "the world" will have this grace. So let us be honest and admit that "poverty" is a relative term.

But our most direct concern is the spiritual reality that the idea of "poverty," or, in fact for most religious, communal property lifts up. It is certainly one the early church thought about and experimented with. Luke records in Acts: "All who believed were together and had all things in common; they would sell their possessions and goods and distribute the proceeds to all, as any had need" (2:44-45). And again: "Now the whole group of those who believed were of one heart and soul, and no one claimed private ownership of any possessions, but everything they owned was in common" (4:32). The early Christians in Jerusalem apparently thought that following Jesus had economic implications. What was this economic experiment about?

First, it was about *koinōnia*, common life, the profound understanding that when persons are baptized into Christ they no longer belong to themselves, but to Christ and *to each other*. For the early church "fellowship" involved not an occasional cozy dinner in the church basement or parish hall with people like themselves, but radical responsibility for other Christians and, beyond that, for suffering people. In both 1 Corinthians and Romans, Paul is very clear that Christians are one body. The implications of this are much more literal and profound than most of us have acknowledged.

Second, it is a practical truth that the more stuff one owns, the more one is owned by one's stuff. Esther de Waal has written: "things carry with them responsibilities."[1] The more things, the more responsibilities. In its best incarnation, refusal to be en-

---

[1] Esther de Waal, *Seeking God: the Way of St. Benedict* (Collegeville: Liturgical Press, 1984) 101.

snared in ownership is intended to open up our horizons, to help us see things from a wider perspective. We have time for others because we are not maintaining our stuff. We are released from the grip of the false values of a consumer and consuming society, from "absorption in the world," which "is the slavery to things."[2] It detaches us and can make us detached.

I am holding up the value of detachment in two senses, both for the end of greater freedom. Detachment from possessions gives us freedom from our immediate circumstances, and so we gain a wider perspective. But we are also called to detachment from the burden of responsibility for the results of our ministries. The call is to be detached from results, and this probably requires some explanation.

In the 1960's Thomas Merton had an extensive correspondence with James Forest who was deeply involved in the peace movement and one of the founders of the Catholic Peace Fellowship. Writing to him on February 21, 1966, Merton says, "Do not depend upon the hope of results. When you are doing the sort of work you have taken on, essentially an apostolic work, you may have to face the fact that your work will be apparently worthless and even achieve no result at all. . . . As you get used to this idea you start more and more to concentrate not on the results but on the value, the rightness, the truth of the work itself."[3] The call is to be openhanded not only with regard to possessions, but to that most dear "possession," the positive results of our apostolic work. Merton's letter to Forest continues: "All the good that you will do will come not from you but from the fact that you have allowed yourself, in the obedience of faith, to be used by God's love."[4] "The real hope . . . is not in something we think we can do, but in God who is making something good out of it in some way we cannot see."[5]

---

[2] Ibid. 102.
[3] William H. Shannon, ed., *The Hidden Ground of Love: The Letters of Thomas Merton* (New York: Farrar, Strauss & Giroux, 1985) 294.
[4] Ibid. 296.
[5] Ibid. 297.

Merton is making a plea for detachment from the burden of responsibility for the results of ministry. And that is so we can be even more radically free people, especially radically free to live in the present moment. And that brings us to Matthew 6, which I am reading as a sort of Christian meditation on detachment.

Structure

A frequently quoted rabbinic proverb states: "By three things is the world sustained: by the Law, by the Temple service, and by deeds of loving kindness."[6] Many scholars have noted that the proverb provides an overall structure for the SM. After the Beatitudes, 5:17-48 is concerned with Jesus' reinterpretation of the Law. If "Temple service" can be understood as a metaphor for worship or personal piety, then 6:1-18 addresses that issue. "Deeds of loving kindness" would include one's attitude toward possessions, the subject of 6:19-34, and most of chapter 7 deals with how we are to treat others.

Our focus in this chapter is 6:19-34, which itself exhibits a clear structure. Three spiritual counsels (which sound like proverbial wisdom) are followed by a poetic exposition of their meaning: first, vv. 19-21 warn about the danger of stockpiling what is impermanent; second, vv. 22-23 are a teaching about seeing (and, at first glance, seem oddly out of place in this context); third, v. 24 is a call to a single focus (much as 5:8 was). Verse 25 picks up from vv. 19-21 and begins the "sermon," if you will, on v. 24. Its theme word is "worry," a term that occurs in vv. 25, 27, 28, 31, 34, and its point is that we should not worry. Let us look briefly at each of these sections and then come back to the notion of detachment.

---

[6] Found in the Mishnah in *ʿAbot* 1 and attributed to Simeon the Just, a Maccabean rabbi.

6:19-21

Douglas Hare has written that "one of the most noticeable characteristics of the human species is its proclivity to collect things . . . . humans everywhere collect 'treasures' and assign status to one another on the basis of what has been acquired."[7] Indeed. Jesus' teaching here is more or less against our acquisitive nature and is not hard to understand. In his world, as in ours, people hoarded things as a way of building a sense of security. The desire for wealth and possessions is really, is it not, a manifestation of a primal kind of fear? And we normally respond to fear by trying to establish security by the nearest available means. "Rust" we understand from the undercarriage of our automobiles! "Moth" was a problem in Jesus' day because fine fabrics were a source of wealth. One might hoard silks or fine linen or the wool of Asia Minor as, today, we hoard money or stock certificates (which, by the way, worms can tunnel in and eat—in fact or in computer viruses!).

Let us be clear that our Lord's point is *not* that material things are evil. This is a great and pervasive misunderstanding. Things are good, or at least neutral, and to be received with thanksgiving, but not served as gods. The point is that material things are impermanent and to hoard them to establish a sense of security is tantamount to "building on sand" as per the final parable in the Sermon (7:25-27). One of the reasons that God's kingdom is hard for the rich to enter is that their hands are already so full. And one tends to trust what is to hand. As Dale Allison has remarked, "empty hands reach out for God; full hands are clutched to the self."[8] Those hands clutched to the self are precisely the opposite image to the open hands, and heart, of detachment, and they are the antithesis of the poor and marginalized of 5:3-6 who are to receive a kingdom and an inheritance.

---

[7] Douglas R.A. Hare, *Matthew*. Interpretation (Louisville: John Knox, 1993) 71–72.

[8] Dale Allison, *The Sermon on the Mount* (New York: Crossroad, 1999) 140.

In terms of revisioning Gospel living, acquisitiveness is an even more important matter, because it deals with the heart's desires. Recall we said that in biblical anthropology the "heart" was the very center of the person, the true self, the core of personality. The practical word of Jesus is that our hearts are turned toward what we treasure. The contrast here is between the earthly, which is not bad because it is earthly or material but because it is impermanent, and the heavenly, which is eternal, permanent. In his book *Thoughts in Solitude* Thomas Merton says two powerful things that shed light on this point: "the things that we love tell us what we are."[9] "Your life is shaped by the end you live for. You are made in the image of what you desire."[10] Justin Martyr said the same thing many years earlier: "Each individual sets his heart on what he counts important, and this allegiance determines the direction and content of his life."[11] The great question is: "to what do we give our hearts?"

6:22-23[12]

On the face of it this seems a rather odd saying to appear in the context of warnings about possessions and security. It seems to reflect the common NT metaphor that "seeing" equals "understanding," but it is a perfect example of the fact that we cannot read the Bible like yesterday's *Times* and interpret it correctly. We need a little lesson in the ancient understanding of eyes and seeing. What we have here is a common expression of how ancient people thought about seeing . . . which is not how we think about it.

---

[9] Thomas Merton, *Thoughts in Solitude* (New York: New Directions, 1956) 22. (Hereafter *TS.*)

[10] Merton, *TS,* 56.

[11] Justin *Apol.* I.15, quoted in David Hill, *The Gospel of Matthew* (Grand Rapids: Eerdmans, 1972) 142.

[12] These are particularly difficult verses. Helpful, but different, readings are given by Dale C. Allison ("The Eye is the Lamp of the Body" [Matt 6:22-23 = Luke 11:34-36], *NTS* 33 [1987] 61–83) and Hans Dieter Betz, ("Matt 6:22-23 and Ancient Greek Theories of Vision," in idem, *Essays on the Sermon on the Mount* [Philadelphia: Fortress, 1985] 71–87).

Ancient people thought the eye was like a lamp that projected inner light onto objects so that they could be seen.[13] Instead of the eye taking *in* light, they thought it gave *off* light or *projected* light so external things could be seen. Imagine the eye giving out a beam of light like a flashlight or torch beam and you've just about got it. The meaning of these verses "is not . . . that a good eye illuminates the body's interior. Rather, when an eye is sound, this shows there is light within. . . ."[14] We all know people whose eyes shine with inner knowledge of God. The ancients did, too, and took what they observed for the literal, optical fact; inner light shone on the outer world. (This way of understanding sight is reflected in John Donne's poetry in which, as they gaze at each other, lovers' "eye beams" are said to intertwine.)

The word for "sound" or "healthy" in v. 22 is *haplous* in Greek. It and its cognates in the LXX "represent the Hebrew root *tam*, meaning 'singleness of purpose,' or 'undivided loyalty,' especially to God. . . ."[15] Its cognates in Hellenistic Greek mean "generous" or "liberal." The idea is a bit obscure, but David Garland clarifies it by saying: "the eye reveals the condition of the heart. Literally, it reads, 'if the eye is single,' which means 'simple' or 'sincere.' The noun form of the word 'single' is used for 'generosity' (Rom 12:8; 2 Cor 8:2; 9:11, 13; Jas 1:5)."[16] So the healthy eye is also the one that, in its singleness of purpose, is generous. (And recall the meaning of "pure" in 5:8.)

These verses are a bit of a puzzle. They are clearly antithetical parallelism, playing off the opposites of healthy/unhealthy eyes. The "healthy eye" has one focus, presumably the "heavenly one" of the immediately previous verses. But a "good eye" is also "generous" and indicates "a proper disposition toward others."[17] Furthermore, in Scripture, God dwells in light and gives light. So

---

[13] M. Eugene Boring, "Matthew," in Leander Keck, et al., eds., *The New Interpreter's Bible* (Nashville: Abingdon, 1995) 210.

[14] Allison, *Sermon,* 143.

[15] Hill, *Matthew,* 142.

[16] David Garland, *Reading Matthew* (New York: Crossroad, 1993) 82.

[17] Allison, *Sermon,* 143.

"darkness" implies separation from God. The unhealthy eye "is the sign of a life engulfed in a darkness that is caused by the lack of generosity with one's possessions (see Prov 23:6-8; 28:22; Sir 14:10; Deut 15:9)."[18] Now we can "see" why these verses appear here. In a sense, they provide a literal rendering of one way those who live the Gospel are "light of the world."

What I think Jesus is getting at is the relationship between "seeing" and "doing." My mother would have said: "if you know better, you do better." Writing in a chapter called "Detachment" in *New Seeds of Contemplation,* Thomas Merton put it this way: "Everything you love for its own sake, outside of God alone, blinds your intellect and destroys your judgment of moral values."[19] In short, inordinate attachment to things causes blindness. Clearly, if the eye is "healthy" it will project good light and help us to see and understand properly. And when we "see" properly, we see the needs of those around us and respond to them. Detachment does not mean indifference. With clear sight comes generosity. The "unhealthy" eye does not see clearly and thus is selfish, perhaps then engaged in the storing up of earthly treasures rather than the dispersal of them to meet human need. Jesus says you can't have it both ways, the point of the next saying.

6:24

This verse is so well known as to be proverbial for us. I think we are no longer shocked that in it Jesus assumes the existence of slavery, which was, after all, the bedrock of the Roman economic system. A slave *was* "mammon" to his or her owner. Jesus envisions a slave who is given contradictory orders by two masters and is thus torn between the two. "Mammon" is simply a Semitic word that means "money" or more generally "possessions." In the context in which we have been speaking, "possessions" seems the most helpful translation. Interestingly, its Hebrew root ʿmn is

---

[18] Garland, *Reading Matthew,* 82.
[19] Thomas Merton, *New Seeds of Contemplation* (New York: New Directions, 1961) 203. (Hereafter *NSC.*)

"used to denote that in which one has confidence."[20] So for Jesus' Aramaic-speaking audience the connection with vv. 19-21 would be self-evident. One stores up mammon, which gives a false sense of confidence. Again, mammon is not, by definition, negative but neutral. Here "mammon" functions as "treasure" did in vv. 19-21. There as here, what matters is what we do with "mammon," what place it has in our scheme of values. The word "hate" (*misesei*) means not only "despise," but "be indifferent to" or "disregard." The verse sums up what has come before it. One must not try to serve both earthly and heavenly treasure. If one "sees" this properly, he or she will act properly toward others, have "healthy sight," be generous.

I think it is so interesting that the spiritual issue, the "Gospel value" in vv. 19-24 is not just money and possessions, but focus. The call is to be "one-focused," to put the kingdom of God before all else, not only to "seek first" the kingdom of God, but to seek *only* the kingdom of God. Thomas Merton put it this way: "If you want to have a spiritual life you must unify your life. A life is either all spiritual or not spiritual at all. No man can serve two masters."[21] Anyone who seriously sets foot on this path toward being one-pointedly "spiritual," a truly "Gospel person," is going to have some anxiety about life's essentials. Jesus knows this and immediately addresses it.

6:25-34

This whole unit is framed by and peppered with the word "anxious" or "worry." I can relate. When a friend who is a Sister and I first traveled together to Ireland in 1993, at the end of the trip she gave me a "worry stone" of Conmarra marble and said, "this was a great trip. I didn't have to worry about anything because you worried about everything!"

In Greek the word "worry" (*merimnate*) means "care for" or "be concerned about," but is also used in the papyri in the sense

---

[20] Hill, *Matthew*, 143.
[21] Merton, *TS*, 56.

of "occupied with" or "employed with." Its root is *meris*, "a part" or "a portion." Do you see the connection with the overall spiritual focus here? Those who worry or are anxious are those who are "parceled out," divided, not unified. In terms of the Beatitudes and our exploration of the term "pure" in 5:8 those who worry are, by definition, not "pure in heart." To store treasure on earth, to be selfish, to serve mammon is to invite anxiety and worry not only because it is the wrong way to seek security, but because it leads to divided loyalty and divided loyalty leads to . . . worry. Vicious circle. First Peter 5:7 gives the cure for the disease, but it is bitter medicine for many of us because it involves giving up the illusion of our own self-sufficiency: "Cast all your anxieties upon him [that is, God], for he cares for you." (And compare Phil 4:6.)

Jesus' "call to tranquillity,"[22] for that is what a warning against worry and anxiety actually is, comes by way of illustrating from the natural world God's care for all creation. Jesus gives examples: birds (v. 26), pointlessness (v. 27), plants (vv. 28-30), and then he makes a very unflattering comparison (vv. 31-33). It is instructive to note that what Jesus' audience is anxious about is not the "extras" of life, but its necessities, enough to eat, something to wear. The context is not our superabundance, our lust for luxury goods, but substance, the basics. I think this makes the teaching much more stark and difficult.

Birds, those unrooted creatures who do not engage in the hard work of farming, are fed by God. Certainly if God cares for the sparrows, as in Matt 10:29 Jesus illustrates God does, God will feed humans? The fruitlessness of worrying is exemplified by the fact that all the worrying in the world won't add a cubit, about 18 inches, to the length of one's life. Birds don't farm, and they are fed. And the grass of the field doesn't spin, but it is clothed. "The 'grass of the field' was a standard image for something that was worthless. Jesus deliberately stresses the paradox between the glorious beauty of the flowers and their final in-

---

[22] Allison, *Sermon*, 146.

significance."[23] In Hebrew Scripture the "grass of the field" is frequently a metaphor for what is transient, short-lived, here today, gone tomorrow. Jesus is asking us to remember how much care God exerts on the most ephemeral of creations. It is not that the birds and the lilies are models to be imitated; they are "powerful symbols of God's providential care."[24]

Jesus uses the natural world, and human nature, to illustrate something about God's nature. And then at v. 32 he says a very harsh thing to the Galilean Jews and to the disciples who are listening, and to us: "only pagans worry like this." The "Gentiles," the *ethnē* or the *goyim*, were *outsiders*, those not included in God's covenant. (Compare 6:7-8, where Gentiles also provide the negative example. Remember that Matthew's Jesus sends the Twelve on mission to "the lost sheep of the *house of Israel*," excluding "pagans" [10:6]. Italics supplied.) My point here is not to stress the Jewishness of Jesus; that is clear enough. What Jesus is saying is that, in fact, the "worry warts" among us are no better than those who don't know God at all! This was standard Jewish teaching. Rabbi Eleazar of Modi'im said that if one had food for the day, but worried "What shall I eat tomorrow?" one was deficient in faith. Similarly, Eliezar the Great said that one who had bread in his basket but worried about what he would eat tomorrow belonged to those of "little faith."[25]

Again the point is not that one should ignore the realities of life, here represented by the need for food and clothing. The point, as v. 33 makes clear, is that these things should not be our reason for living. The disciple's focus is properly the kingdom of God, with its mercy and justice, and the righteousness that is appropriate to living in its reign. Then other things fall properly into place. God's kingdom is the Gospel person's first priority. Jesus is a consummate psychologist. As v. 34 demonstrates, he knows we worry more than anything else about the future. The

[23] Garland, *Reading Matthew,* 83.
[24] Hare, *Matthew,* 74.
[25] Quoted in Allison, *Sermon,* 150.

future was feared by most people in the Greco-Roman world because it was understood to be in the hands of those most capricious of goddesses, the Fates and Fortuna. What Jesus seems to be saying to Gospel people is, "live in the present moment. Address what comes moment by moment and trust the future into the hands of the God who feeds and clothes even the most transient and ephemeral of creations." This call to live in the present moment is its own kind of detachment, a call to detachment from slavery to life's "what if's." And as Dale Allison points out, this text invites us to think about providence "about the special value of human beings, about what it might mean for us to depend on God, and about the possibility that God, despite appearances, is active in the world."[26] Indeed, it is a direct link to the Lord's Prayer and the request "Give us this day our *daily* bread."[27] There is something about having more than the "daily requirement" that Jesus thinks is very bad for us indeed.

The Kingdom Calls for Detachment

Having walked slowly through this second half of chapter 6, let us now go back and consider how the whole chapter is a meditation on detachment and on the meaning of detachment for our re-envisioned Gospel living. What I think the chapter tells us is that poverty is intended to develop in us detachment at the deepest levels of our being, and this detachment is, itself, for the end of freedom. In fact, each vow, in its own way, has greater freedom as its goal. Put negatively, to the degree we are "grasping" or "desiring" we are enslaved. Put positively, to the degree we are detached (not indifferent, but detached), we are free.

The general subject of chapter 5 is intensification of the Torah. Therefore it is not surprising to find Law followed by the "practice of piety." At 6:1 the word translated into English as "piety"

---

[26] Ibid. 151–52.

[27] I know that the Greek word rendered "daily" *(epiousious)* is notoriously difficult to translate and interpret. The point here is not *when* God provides bread, but *that* God can be depended upon to provide what is needed.

is, in fact, *dikaiosunē*, "righteousness," all that is done for human beings to be in proper relationship to God. Here is the link with 5:20. (And compare 5:6, 10.) The old righteousness was understood largely in terms of legal rectitude and ceremonial purity; the new is understood in terms of practical day-to-day behavior, here neatly divided between religious behavior in 6:2-18 and what we might call economic behavior in 6:19-34.

So what has this got to do with detachment? It is introduced at 6:1: do not be pious in front of other people, presumably for the positive response one would receive for such behavior. Appearances, as we all know, are deceiving. Sister sits quietly in front of the Blessed Sacrament and looks so holy when, in fact, she is a holy terror in the kitchen or the laundry! The altar boy looks holy at the altar . . . but is a demon in the classroom. The heavenly reward is for those who practice piety only for God's sake rather than for reward in the form of human approval. And Thomas Merton reminds us that "attachment to spiritual things is . . . just as much an attachment as inordinate love of anything else."[28] Merton thinks it is more harmful because it is more difficult to recognize. Here in Matthew 6, as it was in 5:17-48 and is so often, Jesus' interest is in inner motivation, why we do what we do. The implication, I think, is that we must be detached even from the results of good action. We do what we can, but we leave the results to God.

So the chapter begins with the difficult but crucial matter of spiritual detachment, which is represented by the repeated injunction to practice "in secret" the three traditional aspects of Jewish piety: giving alms, praying, and fasting (6:4, 6, 18). Jesus teaches that spiritual practices are to be carried out in secret for an unseen, spiritual reward. This unseen gift of God leads directly to the question of attachment to earthly things or "earthly treasure" (6:19). I wonder if Jesus associated the two on the basis of this passage from Tobit:

---

[28] Merton, *NSC*, 205–206.

> Prayer is good when accompanied by fasting, almsgiving, and righteousness. A little with righteousness is better than much with wrongdoing. It is better to give alms than to treasure up gold. . . . Those who perform deeds of charity and of righteousness will have fullness of life; but those who commit sin are the enemies of their own lives (Tob 12:8-10).

If you think about it, Matt 6:19-21 urges the "stockpiling" of spiritual treasures (like giving alms, prayer, and fasting). These "heavenly treasures" are "secret," as opposed to those seen by people, things like, well, *things*, wealth, but also titles, education, prestige, family connections, and so on. (Compare Matt 20:25-28; 23:5-12.)

The "soundness" or "health" or "focus" of sight in 6:22-23 has to do with understanding. Right understanding is an extension of "heavenly treasure," and to understand or to "see" rightly is to work toward what is unchanging. To see rightly is to be enlightened, which is literally a gift from heaven, and to enlighten by the active fruit of one's understanding. (Recall 5:14-15.) On the contrary, the attempt to serve two masters in 6:24 is a "darkness" of understanding. Divided loyalty leads to spiritual confusion. Since one cannot serve God and possessions, in 6:25-34 Jesus says, in effect, "forget about serving possessions." God will provide what is needed—not, note, what is *wanted:* necessities, not luxuries.

The issue of "mammon," possessions or money, leads naturally to the list of "earthly treasures" in 6:25-33: food, drink, clothing. These, too, are "seen by people" and are the cause of divisiveness in communities. Who has roast beef for supper and who has canned beans and what does that tell us about them? Who has a fur coat from Lord & Taylor and who has a rain jacket from a discount store and what does that say? (See Jas 2:1-7 for an exposition of this point.) Here, in clear relief, the heavenly and unseen confront the earthly and seen. The point is that God provides *both*; neither is from us or of our doing. Animals and plants are fed and clothed. Animals and plants *provide* food and clothing, and God's generosity makes it all possible.

When we seek God's kingdom and its righteousness (those powerful words in the SM), other things fall into their proper places. "Gentiles" or "pagans" (6:32) seek the seen things (food, clothing), the earthly treasure. To strive for these things is darkness. The heavenly Parent knows we need them and provides them in proportion to our need (and bear in mind that as individuals we have different needs, so it is entirely appropriate that God's provision is not uniform) and to our devotion to God and to heavenly things. So 6:22-24 and 6:32-33 inform each other. But the kingdom and its demands must come first. Both the notion of the kingdom and the ordinal ranking suggest a question of time and, therefore, lead to the summary verse for the chapter: "do not worry about tomorrow, for tomorrow will bring worries of its own. Today's trouble is enough for today" (6:34).

The result of striving, of serving mammon, of laying up treasures and hanging on to them, is anxiety. And anxiety or worry leads to further grasping in a desperate attempt to provide security. It is a vicious cycle. Such fear tightens us up, and, we are now learning, causes all sorts of somatic problems. Detachment loosens us up, makes us healthy and, more to the point, free. The key word is "anxiety," first about being recognized spiritually, seen as pious, and second about being materially provided for. The Greek word *merimnao* is instructive, for it means not only "worry about" or "care for," but "be occupied with" or "be employed with." (See Paul's use in 1 Cor 7:32-35.) Thus the verb very subtly reflects the earthly-seen-impermanent/heavenly-unseen-permanent dichotomy. It also suggests the theme of one focus or one-mindedness that is so important in the SM since its root is related to *merizō*, "to divide," and *meri*, "a part." Anxiety or worry, then, is in direct contradiction to 5:8, 6:24, and 6:33, and the single-mindedness Jesus insists upon. Anxiety projects itself into the future, "tomorrow," and may be about spiritual or material things.

If this is the illness, what is the remedy? I would say we can summarize it by the word "detachment," which means, practically, letting it all go into the hands of God, who, in any case, is already taking care of "it"—whatever "it" is! Merton says simply: "The secret of interior peace is detachment. Recollection is impossible for the man who is dominated by all the confused and changing desires of his own will . . . . even if those desires reach out for the good things of the interior life. . . ."[29] We are freed from anxiety only when we cultivate an attitude of detachment from our securities, whether they be the psychological security of human approval or the material securities of the necessities of life. Jesus promises that we can trust God to provide both when we seek first the kingdom via righteousness.

The story is frequently told of the faithful Christian caught in a flood. A neighbor comes by in a jeep and offers to take him to safety. He replies, "no, I trust God to provide." The waters rise, and people come by in a rowboat and offer to take him to safety. "No, I trust God to provide." Finally, as he clings to the chimney of his house and the waters continue to rise, the Red Cross sends a helicopter to rescue him. He refuses to board it because "God will provide." Shortly thereafter he drowns and goes straight to heaven. He barrels through the Pearly Gates and straight to the Throne of Mercy and confronts God. "I trusted you," he shouts, "Why did you let me drown?" God replies, "I sent a jeep and a rowboat and a helicopter; what more did you want?"

"To seek" the kingdom, of course, is to be actively engaged in the realization of God's righteousness, which is achieved in time through acts of compassion and mercy, but also through acts of justice, working to change the systems that cause suffering and injustice. Detachment is not indifference, especially not indifference to the suffering of others. The great challenge is that we must be detached even from the desire for good results from our seeking what Matthew's Jesus calls "righteousness." In the attitude of detachment and the action of righteousness our Lord shows us how the spiritual life and the work for social justice are one.

One of the particular gifts of detachment that can belong to a re-envisioned Christian or religious life is that of seeing beyond

---

[29] Merton, *NSC*, 207.

our own personal current circumstances. Most of the people in the world have their eyes so firmly fixed on their own concerns that they cannot see, much less appreciate the problems and perspectives of others. To the degree that we are *not* attached to our day-to-day work and ministry, to the degree that we can do it lovingly and with open hands and let it go, to the degree that we can "look up" beyond our own lives and ministries, we are able to provide important perspective and, indeed, spiritual ballast in a world where people are so attached to their own point of view that they are willing to kill those who do not share it.

I think this sort of detachment is what the way of poverty is intended to accomplish. It is intended to open our hands with regard to things so that we can open our hearts with regard to God and people. Writing about poverty in her book *The Way of Simplicity*, Esther de Waal asks: "what does the desire to possess, accumulate do? It will fill up that inner void which keeps a person open to the experience of God."[30] Owning stuff, having all the newest technological toys, is for many people the twisted attempt to fill up what is intended to be the God space within. The interior emptiness is for God alone. Nothing else will satisfy that hunger and that void, certainly not another shopping frenzy.

Detachment, Br. David Steindl-Rast writes, "decreases our needs. The less we have, the easier it is gratefully to appreciate what we do have."[31] The renunciations of poverty, Brother David reminds us, are for greater, more genuine delight. To put it in the terms of this section of the SM, detachment is the means by which we move from earthly to heavenly treasures, not to "own" them, but in order that we can pass *both* on to others. If our detachment is merely for our own salvation, we are no better than the spiritual exhibitionists at the opening of chapter 6.

Let me give the final word to Brother David, who expresses this so much better than I could:

[30] Esther de Waal, *The Way of Simplicity* (Maryknoll, NY: Orbis, 1998) 74.
[31] Bro. David Steindl-Rast, O.S.B., *A Listening Heart* (New York: Crossroad, 1983) 5.

. . . detachment is not a withdrawal from love, but an expansion of love beyond desire. Desire is entangled in time, nostalgic for the past, preoccupied with the future. Love expanding beyond desire is "liberation from the future as well as the past." What remains is the *now* "where past and future are gathered," the "still point."

In our own daily life we may experience the liberating expansion of love. In fact, we may come to find our own actions less and less important, yet . . . even more significant, as the context in which they are seen expands.[32]

Let us pray, in the expansive context of God's love for the whole universe, for detachment, which is the "expansion of love beyond desire."

Questions for Discussion or Further Thought

1. In the light of Two-Thirds World daily realities, in what sense am I/are we "poor"? Realistically speaking, what does "poverty" mean to me/us in economic terms?

2. How is the call to live in the present moment a call to radical detachment?

3. What is the relationship of detachment, as this chapter has presented it, to the needs of others? Can one be too detached from the needs of others . . . or too concerned about them?

4. How would I articulate my own deepest anxieties? What do they tell me about myself? About my relationship to God?

[32] Ibid. 101.

• 4 •

The Kingdom Calls for Humility

Matt 6:10; 7:1-5, 12, 13-14

When we come to the vow of obedience we arrive at what may be the most difficult of the Gospel values to understand and appreciate, both because we bring so much baggage to it and because it has been so massively misunderstood and misapplied. Let us begin by admitting, indeed confessing, that the call to obedience has been badly misused in the Church. Women have been forced to be obedient to patriarchal structures. Men have been brutalized in the name of institutions and nation states. Obedience has been used to secure a mindless conformity in society and within the Church and religious orders and, in the process, has crushed God-given individuality and deformed the inner life of many people. Sometimes this misuse of obedience was well intentioned and sometimes not, but the results are the same: wounded human beings who are less than what God made them to be, less than able to be the salt and light Christ expects them to be.

The really central questions in regard to obedience, it seems to me, are: obedience to what? To what or to whom do I give final allegiance? Who has authority over me and why? Answering such questions requires that we understand the etymological root of the word "obedience." Esther de Waal notes that "obedience" is "derived from the Latin *oboedire*, which shares its roots with *audire*, to hear. So to obey really means to hear. . . ."[1] Brother David Steindl-Rast has written, "Knowledge tries to grasp; wisdom listens. Listening wisdom: that is obedience."[2] Obedience as "listening wisdom" is a fundamental assumption of this chapter because it understands that obedience has to do with what and to whom we listen. Please bear in mind that in the Hebrew Bible "to hear" implied "to obey." If we hear God, we obey God.

Whom do I obey? Who has authority over me and why? These questions lead us directly into the realm of Gospel values in that they remind us of the uncompromising and single-minded loyalty Jesus requires of his disciples. We cannot listen to God and mammon. Nor can we always listen to or be obedient to Christ and to lesser authority figures. The sooner we learn this, the sooner we grow up in the spiritual life.

But, on an entirely different level, today the vow of obedience is perhaps the most profoundly countercultural because it asks us to take ourselves lightly, to understand that we are not the center of the universe. Obedience is for the sake of humility, that most Christ-like of Christian virtues. Over and over again the NT characterizes Jesus Christ by his obedience. (See, for example, Rom 5:19; Phil 2:8, Heb 5:8.) But neither obedience nor humility is highly regarded in our world. Brother David Steindl-Rast quips: "Many think that humility is a pious lie committed by people who claim to be worse than they know themselves to be, so that they can secretly pride themselves in being so humble."[3] Again, we must be careful here because humility must be chosen; it cannot be imposed, and when imposition is attempted, real damage is done. Authentic humility has to do with full personhood and active choice. As Enzo Bianchi has noted:

---

[1] Esther de Waal, *Seeking God: The Way of St. Benedict* (Collegeville: Liturgical Press, 1984) 43.

[2] Brother David Steindl-Rast, O.S.B. *A Listening Heart* (New York: Crossroad, 1983) 107.

[3] Brother David Steindl-Rast, O.S.B., *Gratefulness, The Heart of Prayer* (New York: Paulist, 1984) 202.

"Psychologists understandably prefer the word 'authenticity,' whose meaning is actually quite close to the original meaning of the traditional term *humilitas*."[4] In order for the Gospel value of humility to make sense psychologically I want to begin not with the passages from the SM, but with a reminder about a fundamental christological matter.

Jesus: Model of Humility

Actually, Jesus as model of humility is preceded by Mary model of humility. Like mother, like son! At the root of every fundamentally Christian life is Our Lady's *fiat*: "Here am I, the servant of the Lord; let it be with me according to your word" (Luke 1:38). It is Mary who first models for us the meaning of "Thy will be done." Here is how a contemporary poet put it:

> The Mystery is not
> that God crawled
> into dusty, human flesh,
> but that a village girl child,
> just on the cusp of woman
> had a heart so open
> she could say "yes"
> to its piercing,
> from the shattered bits
> of her plans and dreams
> could nurture one, small shoot.[5]

Another way to define "humility" is to say that it is pliability, malleability in the hands of God. To be humble is to be like Jeremiah's clay. No biblical passage suggests that this is easy. Indeed, all suggest it is costly. And all indicate that in order to "give over" the self for God's purposes one must first fully possess the

---

[4] Enzo Bianchi, *Words of Spirituality* (London: S.P.C.K., 2002) 93.
[5] From "Christmas Rose" in Bonnie Thurston, *Hints and Glimpses* (Three Peaks Press, 2004) 30.

self in a mature way. This is the point I wish to make as we look at the life of Jesus: one must *have* a self in order to choose to relinquish it.

Perhaps the oldest passage in the New Testament is the Christ hymn in Paul's letter to the Philippians, 2:6-11, which I take to be an already existing hymn Paul used illustratively. In this chapter Paul is encouraging the Philippians in their unity as a church. In 2:3 he says: "Do nothing from selfish ambition, or conceit, but in humility regard others as better than yourselves." Now, this is a very difficult command, one that can be badly misunderstood and misapplied. "Selfish ambition" is a political term the Philippians would have understood; it means "factional rivalry." "Humility" would have been the scandalous word to them because it was a slave virtue, not a characteristic proud Roman citizens would have coveted. Greek moralists viewed humility as the subservient attitude of a lower-class person. As here, it involved distasteful self-abasement. The root Greek word *tapeinoō* literally meant "to level a mountain," and that gives important insight into what is being called for when NT writers commend humility. The "mountain" can *choose* to be "made low;" the mighty can *give up* their thrones. What is being commended is not enforced servility or obsequiousness, but chosen service after the model of Christ himself.

No wonder Paul inserts the Christ hymn at this point. Note that the hymn begins by pointing out that Christ was, and knew himself to be, "in the form of God," equal to God (2:6). He was, in Bianchi's terms, fully authentic. He then chooses to empty himself and take a human form, indeed, the lowest human form, the form of a slave, one who has no authority over himself, not even over his own body (2:7). You see the point? It was not that God forced Jesus into some hideous self-abasement but that Jesus, knowing who he was, having possession of himself, *chose* to become human, to die like a slave on the cross. The stunning reality at the heart of the incarnation is that God chose to empty Godself. The Welsh poet R. S. Thomas glimpsed the meaning in his poem "The Coming."

And God held in his hand
A small globe. Look, he said.
The son looked. Far off,
As through water, he saw
A scorched land of fierce
Colour. The light burned
There; crusted buildings
Cast their shadows: a bright
Serpent, a river
Uncoiled itself, radiant
With slime.
            On a bare
Hill a bare tree saddened
The sky. Many people
held out their thin arms
To it, as though waiting
For a vanished April
To return to its crossed
Boughs. The son watched
Them. Let me go there, he said.[6]

Humility has a positive meaning to the degree that it follows exactly the pattern set by Christ. One knows who one is, becomes an
authentic, actualized person, and then one can choose to act on
that basis. "Humility" in the Christian tradition is the virtue describing lowly service chosen and executed by a noble person. It is
best exemplified in the earthly life of Jesus by the foot washing in
John 13 where the "tall one" stoops down of his own accord.

Our gospel writers are not very interested in the sort of psychological motivation that animates most modern literature. So
in the Synoptic Gospels Jesus almost never says very much about
himself, what he is thinking or feeling. A rare exception occurs
in a much-beloved passage in Matt 11:28-30. In this text Jesus
assumes the figure of Wisdom inviting people: "Come to me, all

---

[6] R. S. Thomas, *Poems of R. S. Thomas* (Fayetteville: University of
Arkansas Press, 1985) 82–83.

you that are weary and are carrying heavy burdens, and I will give you rest. Take my yoke upon you, and learn from me; for I am *gentle and humble in heart*, and you will find rest for your souls. For my yoke is easy, and my burden is light." (Italics supplied.) The word Jesus uses to describe himself here is of the same root as the one that appeared in Phil 2:3 and 8. Central to who he is (that is what "heart" signifies, the totality of the self) is the "self-actualized" one who chooses to give his "self" away.

To summarize this point, then, the old vow of obedience was to nurture the Christian virtue of humility. But Christian humility assumes that before we "empty ourselves" or "give ourselves up" we first have full possession of ourselves; we are who we are. Only when I know who I am, when I have glimpsed my ultimate and unique value in the sight of God, can I choose to be humble. Humility as we are speaking of it here is radically *unenforceable*; Christian humility is always chosen or it is not Christian humility. With this in mind, let us return to the SM and to a few passages that give deeper insight into humility so understood.

Matthew 6:10

Let us take just a moment to orient ourselves in the SM again. Recall we said that a Rabbinic proverb suggested that the world was sustained by three things: Torah (Law), worship, and acts of kindness. Chapter 5 of the Sermon is, more or less, on the Law; 6:1-18 deals with piety, and chapter 7 deals with our relationships to one another in a series of imperatives and warnings for the new, Gospel way of life. Jewish piety was characterized by almsgiving, prayer, and fasting, exactly the three subjects Jesus addresses in 6:1-18. The teachings on piety begin with a command to practice "in secret;" 6:1 states the principle of which the following three activities are examples. In each case these actions are to be carried out "in secret" (6:1, 4, 6, 18). This matter of practicing our piety in secret is directly related to the matter of humility. Jesus was interested in motivation in 5:17-48, and that concern continues here. Why are we "being pious"? To be thought well of by others, or to further our relationship to God? What is the motivation for our acts of piety? Sincere desire for God or fear of breaking the liturgical/ecclesiastical rules? The secrecy that is here commanded is a call for both honesty and humility. When we practice "in secret" we are fully open to God—who knows us fully, from whom "no secrets can be hidden," as the Book of Common Prayer puts it.

The Lord's Prayer, then, in 6:9-13, which is the substance of Jesus' teaching on prayer in 6:7-15, is structured not unlike the 10 commandments in that the first three petitions focus on our relationship with God and the last three address human need. Petitions 1 to 3 in Matt 6:9b-10 ask that God's name be sanctified, God's rule be established, and God's will be done. It is this petition, "Thy will be done," that speaks to the virtue of humility because implicit in it is the understanding that something other than my *own* will should direct my life.

The reign of God for which we pray in the second petition is closely connected to the will of God in this petition. (Recall what we said about "kingdom of God/heaven" in the introduction to the Beatitudes.) Where God's reign is, God's will is done. This is what it means for God's kingdom to come: God's will is fulfilled to the exclusion of all others, even mine! Jan Lochman has pointed out that submission to God is the supreme virtue and freedom of Christians.[7] Here, again, we must return to the example of Jesus as the one who most perfectly did God's will. The writer of the Hebrew letter says Christ came into the world and said "I have come to do your will, O God" (10:7). In John's gospel Jesus says: "for I have come down from heaven, not to do my own will, but the will of him who sent me" (6:38). In the anguish of the Garden of Gethsemane Jesus prayed "your will be done" (Matt 26:42). William Barclay goes so far as to say that obedience to God's will was the "ruling principle of Jesus' own life."[8] And it is worth noting that even Jesus had to struggle toward it.

[7] Jan Lochman, *The Lord's Prayer* (Grand Rapids: Eerdmans, 1990) 68.
[8] William Barclay, *The Lord's Prayer* (Louisville: Westminster John Knox, 1998) 66.

When we pray "Thy will be done," presumably we include ourselves in the bargain. We are asking, consciously or not, that God's will be done in *us*. And that is a prayer for the radical humility of Jesus. When we pray that God's will be done in heaven and on earth we admit that the doing of God's will is to be understood in an absolute sense. It is in *my* life that God's will must be supreme, in *my* choices and decisions. When we pray this petition, Tertullian suggested we are not only submitting to God's will, but asking for the strength and capacity to do it. In the *Didache* early Christians were taught to pray this prayer three times daily, which is an implicit recognition that God's will is not done among us Christians and a thrice daily reminder to submit to it. Personally, I find this to be a recognition of my lack of humility, of my self-assertion. In short, "thy will be done" is a radical prayer for personal humility in that it assumes my plans and programs are to be entirely set aside in favor of God's plans and programs, what we call the "kingdom of God." And that has profound public and social implications, for it means that because of this kind of humility we are best positioned to bring about the changes that the reign of God will require.

Matthew 7:1-5

Matthew 7:1-5 is part of a longer section of the SM, 6:19–7:12, about what Dale Allison calls "social obligations."[9] It "corresponds to the third of the Three Pillars of Judaism, 'Deeds of loving kindness'" and "resembles proverbial wisdom."[10] The opening "do not judge" "hooks the attention of the listener because it challenges an everyday, taken-for-granted activity."[11] Let us be honest. We all judge, and we spend a lot of our waking thought and energy doing so! Verses 1-5 are a call to humility in

---

[9] Dale C. Allison, *The Sermon on the Mount* (New York: Crossroad, 1999) 138.

[10] M. Eugene Boring, "The Gospel of Matthew," in Leander E. Keck, et al., eds., *The New Interpreter's Bible* (Nashville: Abingdon, 1995) 209.

[11] David Garland, *Reading Matthew* (New York: Crossroad, 1993) 85.

the context of building a compassionate Christian community and warn us of the danger of this sort of judgementalism. On a deep level these verses speak to us of humility as honest knowledge of ourselves, our own faults.

These verses are so well known as to need little commentary. Allison gets it just right when he says that "human beings unhappily possess an inbred proclivity to mix ignorance of themselves with arrogance toward others."[12] Judgmentalism is "a disease of the spirit."[13] And, as Douglas Hare notes, especially in Matthew's gospel "it is expressive of ingratitude."[14] Since God has been so gracious in forgiving us, Matthew's Jesus expects us to forgive each other, as the petition in 6:12 (and its gloss in 6:14-15) and his parable in Matt 18:23-35 so dramatically illustrate.

On the level of Gospel living, of Christian spirituality, judgmentalism is a manifestation of that most dangerous of sins, pride, overstepping the boundaries of our humanity. T. W. Manson has noted that "judging persons is in God's hands, for He alone knows the secrets of men's hearts."[15] While I stumble over Manson's exclusive language here, his point is entirely well taken. Most of the time I hardly know myself, my own deepest motivations. How can I presume to know those of others? The point of Matt 7:1-5 is that people who judge others do not know themselves very well. The word "hypocrite" (one of Jesus' favorite negative terms in Matthew's gospel) literally means one who pretends to be other than he or she is. The verb for "see" in v. 3 which alludes to the neighbor's "speck" connotes merely physical apprehension. But the verb for "see" in v. 5, which commands first "looking to" ourselves, means "see clearly" or "see accurately."

These verses do not rule out any and every kind of judgment. What they do is to set a priority. Judge self first, then others

---

[12] Allison, *Sermon*, 153.

[13] Douglas R. A. Hare, *Matthew*. Interpretation (Louisville: John Knox, 1993) 76.

[14] Ibid. 77.

[15] Quoted in Allison, *Sermon*, 152.

when you are, yourself, fully clearsighted. The Greek word "judge" (*krinō*) has as part of its lexical meaning "to decide," "to consider," what we might mean by "discern." Thus it is related to the root meaning of "obedience" as "listening toward." To judge ourselves first is to practice true humility, true knowledge of who we are and who we are not. It means listening carefully to ourselves and our own motivations. We learn who we are by listening to ourselves in the silence of our hearts. What the Jesuits call "consciousness examine," which is, in part, an honest appraisal of my own shortcomings, is not for the purpose of making me feel bad and inadequate. Nobody needs to help most of us beat up on ourselves; we do that quite well, thank you very much! Most fundamentally, self-judgment is to develop my compassion toward others. As Esther de Waal says: "Knowing my own limitations I have no right to destroy other people for theirs."[16]

How important the matter of what I call "the humility of silence" is in community life, whether the "community" is a religious order, a family, or a parish! Certainly one primary way we can practice humility is to be silent when we might speak some word of judgment or criticism. We can be very edifying by our silences, especially when those around us are involved in a "roast" of somebody else. Jesus has reminded us that there is no greater love than to give our lives for our friends (John 15:13). One way to "give up our lives" is to give up the tendency to judgment, for, let us be honest, judging others is a way, albeit a terrible and misguided way, to feel better about ourselves. *We* are good. *They* are flawed. *We* are good. *They* are evil. Such polemical and exclusionary rhetoric is particularly divisive in the present political and religious climate. It is recorded that the desert Father, Abbot Moses, said: "A man ought to be like a dead man with his companion, for to die to one's friend is to cease to judge him in anything."[17] And this brings us, in a roundabout

[16] de Waal, *Seeking God*, 47.
[17] Quoted in Thomas Merton, *The Wisdom of the Desert* (New York: New Directions, 1960) 75.

way, to the "Golden Rule," for we do not judge because we do not want to *be* judged.

Matthew 7:12

Several commentators have noted that 7:12 stands alone as a summary of Jesus' understanding of the Law. As such, it marks off chapter 7 of the SM into two sections: (1) 7:1-11 dealing with judging (7:1-5), sharing the gospel (7:6), and asking and receiving (7:7-11), and (2) 7:13-27 setting forth, in Eugene Boring's happy turn of phrase, two ways (7:13-14), two harvests (7:15-23), and two builders (7:24-27).[18] Additionally, 5:17 and 7:12 both refer to Jesus' view of "the law and the prophets," and may indicate an inclusion that brackets 5:17–7:12 "as the instructional body of the sermon."[19]

In the context of living Gospel values, we can easily see how the "Golden Rule" speaks of the reciprocity and "indiscriminate" (in the sense of not making distinctions between people) quality of humility. Such "indiscrimination" also characterizes God according to Acts 10:34; God shows no partiality, has no favorites. (This point also stands behind Jesus' parable in Matt 20:1-16.) When we see ourselves as we are, we understand that we should treat others as we wish to be treated because "they are us." This "Golden Rule" is not unique to Jesus' teaching; it occurs in several places in Jewish literature and in the teaching of many other of our world's wisdom figures. As C. S. Lewis has said, "Really great moral teachers never do produce new moralities. It is quacks and cranks who do that."[20]

That it is not a unique teaching does not make it any easier to live out. To treat others as we would be treated is a life principle deeply rooted in the commonality of human life, in the recognition of our fundamental likeness in the human family. And this is

---

[18] Boring, "Matthew," 213–19.

[19] Ibid. 213.

[20] Quoted in Archibald M. Hunter, *A Pattern for Life: An Exposition of the Sermon on the Mount* (Philadelphia: Westminster, 1953) 22.

the root of humility as well, which shares its linguistic meaning with *humus*, dirt, the fundamental stuff of which we are all made. As Br. David Steindl-Rast notes, "to be humble means simply to be earthy."[21] So much for the unearthly false piety that tries to pass itself off as humility! Humility begins when we accept and embrace the earthiness of our human condition. That would, imply, it seems to me, an embrace of all of incarnate life, beginning with our own bodies. So humility is related to charity. Esther de Waal speaks of humility as being "profoundly earthed,"[22] and that is a helpful turn of phrase. Jesus calls me to treat others as I would want to be treated precisely because I am as they are, made of the same stuff. We are "grounded together" in God's creating and creative love.

To put the matter very simply, the Gospel value of humility, here expressed as "behavioral reciprocity," calls us to give up the desire for prestige and position, the little things that might indicate we are "superior" to others. Marking our difference from others is profoundly bred into us from the time we are children. Even scholars seem to covet the little ribbons on conference name tags that say "presenter" or "speaker." It marks us off from the *hoi polloi* at the meeting! Knowing where we fit on the social scale, the intellectual achievement grid, the economic pecking order is often part and parcel of the creation of a "false self." We have a perverse tendency to define ourselves in relationship to others rather than in the discovery of our own uniqueness. I think this is why Matthew's Jesus forbids the use of honorary titles like "Teacher" (Rabbi, 23:10). Titles like Father, Sister, and Doctor separate those who insist on them from our common humanity; they elevate some and "demote" others. Let us be honest. Mostly we don't want to be treated like others; we want to be treated better than they are. This is a profound falsity, as Jesus' own life demonstrated.

---

[21] Steindl-Rast, *Gratefulness*, 203.
[22] de Waal, *Seeking God*, 45.

Matthew 7:13-14

Because humility is the characteristic virtue of Christian life, a virtue that is hard won for most of us, that life itself is envisioned by the Lord as a "narrow way." The instructional form of the "two ways," which we see in 7:13-14, is a very common one in Judaism (see, for example Deut 30:19 or Jer 21:8), was enthusiastically appropriated in early Christian catechesis, and occurs in many of the world's great wisdom traditions. The comparison in 7:13-14 is between wide and easy, narrow and hard. "Easy" and "hard" are more nearly opposites in Greek than they appear in English. The Greek word "easy" (*eurychōros*) actually means "spacious, roomy" while "hard" (*tethlimmenē*) means "pressed together," that is, not spacious or roomy.[23] "Hard" derives from a word that means "press" and has the metaphorical sense of "oppress," "afflict," or "distress." "Since the Greek word for 'narrow' . . . can also be used metaphorically with the meaning 'troubled' or 'beset with difficulty,' it is possible that Matthew's first readers understood the statement as reminding them that the Christian way involves misunderstanding, rejection, and persecution. Those who strive to do what is right, instead of adhering to a lowest-common-denominator morality, must not expect to receive popular acclaim. . . ."[24] Alas. No popular acclaim accrues to the humble, but they, like the meek in 5:5, are promised the earth.

Jesus is ever the realist. He does not want us to misunderstand the difficulty of the life to which he calls us. First, it will not be the way that everyone will go. To use a modern metaphor, "the many" may race madly on the highway; we who seek to live by Gospel values are called to the meandering, narrow, back ways. But second, there is an implied note of hope here. The call to Gospel life is a "way." It is a path or a road, a process that proceeds from an initial decision. The Gospel call is not to a static state but to a dynamic journey. (Remember the discussion

---

[23] David Hill, *The Gospel of Matthew* (Grand Rapids: Eerdmans, 1984) 150.

[24] Hare, *Matthew*, 82.

of "perfect" in 5:43-48. And recall that the Synoptic Gospels all have a journey narrative in which Jesus teaches discipleship.) To continue the metaphor, if we fall or take a wrong turn on this way we are not abandoned by the side of the road, but encouraged to get up, dust off, and continue the journey. And that dust that we've fallen in is the best possible reminder of who we all are!

The Kingdom Calls for Humility

Finally, then, what is the deep, Gospel call of obedience and the virtue of humility to which it calls us? Paradoxically, I think it is freedom. First, humility liberates us from the slavery of thinking of ourselves at the center of our own life and of life in general. How many people can only look at issues from their own point of view, only see an action from the standpoint of how it affects them! Humility is a call to see our common-ness, our humanity, indeed, a clarion call to give up the selfishness at the root of all sin. Humility, understood in the terms we have been considering, may well be the "cure" for the alienation of our age.

Writing of obedience in the Rule of St. Benedict, Esther de Waal goes to the heart of the matter when she says: "obedience means that I lay aside idols, and empty myself at my centre, so that I can reach out to others."[25] "Obedience is really about love. . . . The outcome of obedience . . . is that it brings with it an inner freedom."[26] What humility asks us to deal with is self-will that nearly always manifests itself as self-centeredness. And self-centeredness is a terrible, terrible kind of slavery. The most radical call of the Gospel is a call to live as Jesus lived, to live for God and for others, and in that process to be fully liberated and free with the freedom Christ died to give us. (See Gal 5:1.)

More paradoxically still, obedience and its end, humility, free us from the servitude of an unexamined life. The real point of

---

[25] de Waal, *Seeking God*, 119.
[26] Ibid. 44.

obedience is not to do someone else's will but to be who God created us to be. God did not make us to be like everybody else. The ridiculous conformity of consumerism, of "fashion," and all that advertising tells us we should be and wear and own, is in contradistinction to who God created the human person to be. The calls to humility and to detachment are closely related. Being detached from things, especially the false needs that advertising seeks to create in us, exercises the muscles of humility. Humility, paradoxically, is individuating. In refusing to become part of the consuming herd we become persons. We were not created on an assembly line for the purpose of collecting stuff made on assembly lines. Not only is there in each one of us, as St. Augustine understood, an emptiness that only God can fill, there is an "emptiness" in God, a "space" or a "shape" in the Divine Purpose that only each one of us as person fully realized can fill. Mind you, this is a metaphor and an imperfect one, but it is the best I can do. God meant us to be individualized for God's purposes in creation and redemption. And the way we most clearly find this "way" is to recognize our common humanity.

Writing about humility, Enzo Bianchi, founder of the ecumenical community at Bose, said humility is "our courageous *acceptance of who we are in front of God.*"[27] Humility "is authentic self-knowledge, it wounds our narcissism, because it leads us back to who we really are—that is, to our *humus*, our identity as created beings."[28] Thomas Merton said "the saint is unlike everybody else precisely because he is humble."[29] He continued, "humility consists in being precisely the person you actually are before God."[30] This is perhaps the best definition of humility I have ever encountered: it is being who I am before God, no masks, no pretense, no pretending to be better or worse than I am. Being me. Because me is who God made to fill the

[27] Bianchi, *Words of Spirituality*, 94.
[28] Ibid.
[29] Thomas Merton, *New Seeds of Contemplation* (New York: New Directions, 1961) 99.
[30] Ibid.

"me shape" in God and in the divine plan, to fulfill the bit of the task that is mine in bringing the kingdom of God into being. I am that important. And so are you. And so is everybody. And the call of humility is the call to live like it.

Questions for Discussion or Further Thought

1. In what ways was I/am I abused by misguided obedience imposed from without or misguided humility imposed from within?

2. The call to humility is a call to commonality, to see ourselves as like others. What does this mean for me as an individual/for us as a community?

3. We have been presented with the idea that humility is for freedom. Do I/we agree with this? What, practically, might it mean for me/us?

4. What emotions does the word "humility" elicit in me? What do these emotions (indeed, perhaps my own visceral reaction) tell me?

• 5 •

Monasticism and Marriage[1]

History has demonstrated that monasticism, and the various forms of religious life that have grown from it, is an important expression of Christian life and one of the most vital ways in which Christian faith has found expression. It is not necessarily *the* best way, and certainly not the only way. Commitment to this form of life arose in an era when the Christian world was becoming materially powerful and affluent, but spiritually hungry and morally bankrupt. "Religious life" (and although I know the two are not, strictly speaking, the same, I am using this term synonymously with historic monasticism) was a reaction to social disruption and laxity within the Christian community. Its impetus came from a desire to live the Gospel life. To this extent monasticism as a Christian vocation has important lessons to teach all serious and sincere Christians. Monasticism is one of the outward and visible manifestations in church history of

[1] In the spring of 1996 I was honored to give a McManis Lecture at Wheaton College. The series was on "Recovering an Evangelical Spirituality," and I lectured on monasticism and marriage. A good deal of this chapter comes from that lecture, and I am grateful for permission to use it here and to Professor Alan F. Johnson of Wheaton and to the students who were so attentive, engaged, and hospitable during my visit.

81

God's call to holiness of life. It is an "alternative lifestyle" that has called some men and women for the love of Jesus to lives of poverty, chastity, obedience, and stability, virtues that, I would argue, are in precious short supply in our world and desperately needed.

My point is not to glorify religious life but to commend the Gospel values it has, at its best, embodied. I am certainly not suggesting that we should all become monks or brothers or nuns, but in at least four areas religious life holds up spiritual values that should be dear to the hearts of all Christians. First, Holy Scripture and common worship are central to the monastic and traditionally religious life. The monastic vocation radically affirms and accepts a serious interpretation of the teachings and example of Jesus Christ and has historically made the worship of God the central and most important activity of "life together." The Bible was so crucial to early monastics that monks and nuns were called upon to memorize large portions of it before being accepted into communities. Second, the monastic vocation has been suspicious of materialism. Avarice, greed, mindless acquisition, affluence are quietly questioned by traditional religious life. The widespread and erroneous "health and wealth" preaching and teaching that is passed off in middle America as the Gospel is radically challenged by the monastic way.

Third, and related to the second, the monastic/religious vocation places high value on work in and for the community. As a corrective to the rugged individualism of the American myth, monasticism and religious life hold forth the value of work for the sake of the common good and embody Paul's injunction to the Philippians, "each of you should look not only to your own interests, but also to the interests of others" (Phil 2:4). This attitude toward work is intended to prevent it from becoming an end in itself, an idol to which everything else in life bows down. In her book on the Benedictine way written for lay persons like herself, wife and mother Esther de Waal notes, "a safeguard that St. Benedict builds into his community is that work is to be done in a communal context. . . . This is both a check against unconscious pride and against overwork."[2] Most of us ordinary Christians, especially those of us influenced by the Puritan work ethic, work too hard and play too little. The call of the Benedictine way, and of most religious rules, is a call to balance in life, to work for the community's sake, but also to pray and to play, to rest, to recreate.

Fourth, the religious life has always had special concern for the dispossessed, concern for care of the sick, the weak, the stranger. Long before the Jesuit Fathers issued their call for the "preferential option for the poor," religious embodied it as they reached out to meet human need, staffed and built hospitals and orphanages and schools. Hospitality, broadly understood as welcoming and providing for all the people God loves, has always been a monastic virtue. It exemplifies the social action and social service that are appropriately part of Christian spiritual life.

In what follows I want to apply this reflection on religious life to another form of Christian vocation and common life, the vocation of marriage. The unfortunate divorce (if you will pardon the word) between monasticism and marriage as ways of living actually originates in the New Testament period. The Essene community in the Judean desert apparently encouraged the severing of the bonds that tied people to the material world in order that they might more freely serve God. The Essene documents say the community did not marry (although female skeletons were found in their cemetery). And Greek culture, which so influenced early Christianity, favored asceticism, and ascetics claimed special spiritual endowments. The unencumbered life of the early disciples of Jesus, both males and females, led to the acceptance of asceticism and celibacy as principles of virtuous life in the early church. And Paul's teaching on marriage, in fact, often led to a "double standard" with regard to Christian vocation. Marriage was sanctioned, "acceptable," but singleness and celibacy were understood to be better. (See, for example, 1 Cor 7:1-2, 7a in which marriage is concessionary.)

---

[2] Esther de Waal, *Seeking God: the Way of St. Benedict* (Collegeville: Liturgical Press, 1984) 110.

But there are ways in which, on the spiritual level, I would want to suggest that the radical disjuncture between these two ways of life is, in fact, forced. Ideally, religious life and marriage both are entered into as calls from God, not passively drifted into without consideration and conviction. Both are vocations, a calling to spiritual perfection that is freely chosen and a vowed mode of Christian life. It is worth remembering that both marriage and religious life begin with the taking of vows before God, solemn and binding promises. The quest for personal transformation in Christ leads some to the choice of religious life, and the same ought to be said of Christian marriage. Perhaps the appalling rate of divorce is in part because marriage is not taught and understood as "call" or a "vowed life." I suggested that monasticism has served a prophetic function in the church, calling persons radically to follow Jesus. Christian marriage, too, has a prophetic function to bear witness in the church and to the world of the love of Christ, to be a visible symbol and reminder of Christ's love for the church.[3] Certainly this is how the writer of Ephesians understood it in 5:21-33 (especially vv. 29-33).

According to Clement of Alexandria (ca. 215 C.E.) marriage is "the common way of life willed by God for procreation of children." The most common form of western religious life is cenobitic, a word formed from the Greek root *koinos*, "common," and *bios*, "life." Both marriage and religious life are built on a life in common for the sake of greater life. Both include sharing with others the necessities of that life. Both are intended to form persons so called into great Christlikeness and to open them to the kingdom that is to come. In the Rule of Benedict there is a "middle way" that provides the potential for a shared spirituality. Benedict's approach to the daily realities of human life moved the ascetic, monastic ideal into the realm of the possible for married persons. The vows of traditional monastic life— poverty, chastity, and obedience—and the touchstones of Bene-

---

[3] H. V. Sattler, "Marriage, theology of," *New Catholic Encyclopedia* (New York: McGraw-Hill, 1967) 9:266.

dictine monastic spirituality, stability, and hospitality, can, and I think should, characterize Christian marriage. It is to those five virtues, three of which we have examined in light of the Sermon on the Mount, that I wish now to turn, specifically with a view to suggesting ways in which the monastic or religious vow can inform Christian marriage.[4]

Poverty

As I am thinking of poverty here, it is a "lifestyle choice," not the evil of involuntary impoverishment or economic disadvantage or the knee-jerk, unexamined life of conspicuous consumption that is at the root of so many modern economies. It has its origins in the teaching of Jesus: "Do not store up for yourselves treasures on earth. . . . For where your treasure is, there your heart will be also" (Matt 6:19, 21); ". . . it is hard for a rich man to enter the kingdom of heaven" (Matt 19:23). Luke's first Beatitude is unspiritualized: "Blessed are you who are poor, for yours is the kingdom of God" (Luke 6:20). Jesus knew that undue attachment to the things of this life could block our way to the greater life he came to give. (See discussion of this point in Chapter Three.) Indeed, it could be a particularly terrible servitude.

Jesus says the poor will always be with us (Mark 14:7), but he does not suggest this is a good thing, or that poverty *per se* is good. It isn't. Inequitable distribution of goods that allows the rich to become richer while the poor suffer want is, pure and simply, evil. (See the book of Amos.) Benedict, too, realized that poverty that left people hungry and cold interfered with the work of the Spirit in their lives. In his communities Benedict allowed a pound of bread and a quarter liter of wine per day per monastic, amounts that would leave some of us overweight and drunken. Benedict wanted his monks and nuns well fed enough to be able to pray and to serve well the community and those

---

[4] Some of this material appeared in my article, "Monasticism and Marriage," *Contemplative Review* 17/4 (1984) 6–12.

outside it. The vow of poverty in both monastic and married life really asks us to examine the overall orientation of our lives. For what end are we living?

What, then, do I mean by poverty as a monastic virtue or a Gospel value in marriage? Dorothy Day puts it this way: ". . . in a world of enslavement through installment buying and mortgages, the only way to live in any true security is to live so close to the bottom that when you fall you do not have far to drop, you do not have much to lose."[5] Attachment to material security is at the root of many marriages, and it is a poor foundation upon which to build. While considering the lilies of the field (Matt 6:25-34) seems naïve, it is exactly what Jesus asks us to do, and it may save our marriages. How many marriages would be happier if both parents didn't feel they had to work to provide more "things," or if the primary breadwinner could work less? How many fewer strokes, heart attacks, and stress-related illnesses would there be?

Not only are we to avoid undue desire for and anxiety about material things, more radically even than that, we must realize that what we have and hold on to over and above what we need, we are stealing from others. Again, Dorothy Day: "We *are* our brother's keeper. Whatever we have beyond our own needs belongs to the poor."[6] Strong words! The materially blessed bear responsibility for others not so fortunate, for the children of families where both parents *must* work to feed, clothe, and house themselves (not for luxury goods and the newest technological toys), for one-parent families, for the unemployed and underemployed and, especially, Scripture would suggest, for these people within the "household of faith." Within the Christian community there is still a world of practical wisdom in the seldom-practiced passage in Acts 2:43-47. Because the early Christians were, by and large, poor *and* generous, they had the favor of God and of the people, and for this reason God added

---

[5] Dorothy Day, "A Strange and Elusive Thing," *Sojourners* 11/1 (1982) 22–23.

[6] Ibid.

to their numbers, according to Luke. It is quite clear in the New Testament that Christian *koinōnia* included a measure of financial responsibility for other Christians.

The spirituality of poverty in marriage must lead to shutting off television and advertising's world of "bigger and better," "newer and improved," and "more for me." (It may call us to pull the plug on the TV altogether.) The call of poverty in marriage asks us to develop desires born in a stable, not on Madison Avenue. It is certainly a call to a principle of moderation in our economic lives: neither want nor affluence, enough, but not more. Such a principle of marital poverty is intended to free us from slavery to things. It must lead us to greater self-sufficiency in the sense of "making do" in order to be able to share our resources more fully. It must teach us to rejoice in enough rather than in luxury. Consider that our affluent, high-on-the-food-chain life is literally killing all of us on the planet: us from overindulgence; others from want of basic necessities; the earth itself from pollution. Marital poverty as suggested here, consciously chosen by both parties in the marriage (and including children to the degree that it can be explained to them), can lead us to be more informed about real need in the world and how we can address it by beginning first with our own patterns of consumption.

Those attempting the virtue of poverty in Christian marriage can learn from religious life and monastics. This is nicely summarized in the *Rule of Taizé*: "The spirit of poverty is to live in the gladness of today."[7] Tomorrow will, indeed, take care of itself if we are doing what we are supposed to be doing today. Daring to live "close to the bottom" teaches this lesson, as does gratitude for the graciousness of the God who provides.

Chastity

On the face of it, it may seem odd to speak of chastity in marriage. But I think it is an important issue to raise, not because

[7] *The Rule of Taizé* (New York: Seabury, 1968) 19.

marriage is a license to have sex (gone are the days when that was the case!), but because marital chastity, first of all, has to do with fidelity. The first vow that Christian couples traditionally make to each other is "forsaking all others, be faithful to him/her as long as you both shall live." A faithful marriage is one of trust and honesty, one that realizes the great freedom of knowing what the boundaries are. I think it's a good thing that sexuality has been brought out into the open for frank consideration. So long as we are doing so, let us older married people witness to younger couples that sexual exclusivity in marriage is a blessing that allows the relationship to blossom and deepen, that allows for the two to become more fully one, and that, not coincidentally, can lead to great sex. Many recent studies have shown that married people not only have intercourse more frequently than "swinging singles," but are more satisfied sexually.

Marital chastity has little to do with abstinence. Paul does allow brief periods of abstinence for spiritual reasons, "by mutual consent and for a time, so that you may devote yourselves to prayer. Then come together again so that Satan will not tempt you because of your lack of self-control" (1 Cor 7:5). The word "chastity" comes from the Latin root *castus,* which means "pure" or "innocent." Marital sexuality was intended by God to be as innocent as that of Adam and Eve in the Garden of Eden, who were naked and unashamed. Marital chastity suggests, then, avoidance of whatever would debase, cheapen, or make tawdry "innocent sex." Pornography, practices both parties cannot fully enjoy, forced intercourse (rape within marriage), as well as cheating on one's spouse are excluded by marital chastity, which is the glory of human sexuality and the celebration of sexual love that is part of God's great design for procreation and for human pleasure and fulfillment.

Being pure and innocent in married chastity is not being prudish or squeamish about the body and its functioning. Nor is it simply avoiding adultery or pornography or a "dirty magazine mentality." It is an attitude toward one's spouse and one's self that is characterized by respect and generosity and a sense of humor (because sex can be very, very funny). Nor is passion the opposite of marital chastity; it is intrinsic to it, a celebration of it. Many people are afraid of passion, and on some level that is not only a transgression against chastity but a refusal of incarnation, of life in the body God made and proclaimed good.

The Book of Common Prayer of the Episcopal Church includes in the prayers offered for the new couple at their marriage this petition: "Make their life together a sign of Christ's love to this sinful and broken world, that unity may overcome estrangement, forgiveness heal guilt, and joy conquer despair."[8] Christian marriage is intended to point beyond itself, to make two people so secure in love that they can reach out to others. As Richard Rohr writes, it "is a school, a sacrament, a promise of the coming kingdom, but not itself the final stage. Jesus dethroned married love in order to enthrone it in proper perspective. The specific love points to the universal."[9] Chastity as a monastic virtue for marriage, a Gospel value for married persons, involves faith, purity, respect, and a clear understanding that it must not be our spouses, but our Lord who holds first place in our hearts. That said, in a Christian marriage, in one's spouse's heart, second place is a great place to be.

Obedience

In Chapter Four we have already considered many of the difficulties inherent in the vow of obedience as it was traditionally understood. Of all the Christian virtues, obedience would probably universally win the unpopularity context. In the context of Christian marriage I am sorry to say that I think this is because the predominantly male clergy (I am thinking here of all Christian denominations) have not read and studied deeply enough in the Pauline and Petrine letters to understand that "submission" is

---

[8] *The Book of Common Prayer* (New York: Oxford University Press, 1979) 429.

[9] Richard Rohr, "Reflections on Marriage and Celibacy," *Sojourners* 8/5 (May 1979) 22.

a two-way street. Thankfully, excellent contemporary biblical scholarship is changing this narrowness, and we are beginning to hear more exhortation along the lines of Peter's "*all of you*, live in harmony with one another; be sympathetic, love as brethren [(Greek *philadelphoi*, my translation)], be compassionate and humble" (1 Pet 3:8, italics supplied).

Christian marriage does not make one partner master and the other slave. Both partners are to be obedient to God, who is their mutual "master." Within this context obedience is a direct outgrowth of humility, as Chapter Four tried to suggest. Thomas Merton writes about monastic humility in a way that is illuminating for marital spirituality.

> The victory of monastic humility is the full acceptance of God's hidden action in the weakness and ordinariness and unsatisfactoriness of our own everyday lives. It is the acceptance of our own incompleteness, in order that [God] may make us complete in [God's] own way. . . . It is peace in our own unfruitfulness which [God] . . . makes immensely fruitful without our being able to understand how it is done.[10]

The practice of humble obedience to God, and then to each other, occurs in ordinary and sometimes unsatisfactory circumstances in our marriages. It teaches us that our perfection is to be worked out not on our own terms, but together and as part of the gift of the other who shows us to ourselves in ways we might never otherwise envision . . . or even wish to see. And in seeing our strengths, and our incompleteness, in loving relationship, by obediently striving to amend our faults and shortcomings, we become more fruitful and loving persons. Self-will interrupts the process, a self-will that Merton thinks leads ultimately to fear, anxiety, and spiritual slavery.[11]

Putting the matter simply, obedience is really about love, for God and for each other. To experience love, I must be willing to

---

[10] Thomas Merton, *The Silent Life* (New York: Dell, 1959) 21.
[11] Ibid. 47.

give my self away. And that, of course, as we suggested earlier, assumes a fully formed and appropriated "self" to give. Clinging to self, to "me" and "mine" in temperament, actions, and thoughts prevents one from being pliable and obedient to God's will. The *Rule of Taizé* reminds us, "Perfect joy is in the laying aside of self in peaceful love."[12]

I am certainly not going to suggest that this is always easy or pleasant. My own experience as a wife was that it was not. My first real marital struggle with obedient humility and self-giving, ironically enough, was tied to the issue of poverty. It had to do with putting my husband's name on the tiny (and I mean minuscule!) savings account I'd scrimped to save while in graduate school. That money was important to me. And it was symbolic. It represented individualistic control over my own life. I knew in my head that was an illusion, but it was not easy to turn it over to mutual, rather than individual, decision making.

Nothing in our society encourages or rewards the mutual obedience that arises from humility. Modern wives are sneered at for being obedient in this way to their husbands. Modern husbands are taunted by "the boys" for mutual submission to their wives. But the paradigmatic example of this kind of self-giving love is nothing other than the love of Christ as we see it on the cross. "This self giving," suggests the *Rule of Taizé*, "implies the acceptance of a sensibility often deeply wounded."[13] "There is no love of one's neighbor without the Cross. The Cross alone makes known the unfathomed depths of love."[14] Monastic and marital obedience have little to do with jurisdiction, power, and control, and everything to do with mutual submission to the will of God for every human life as that is seen in Jesus Christ. As in the Gospel values of poverty and chastity, obedience is not primarily to be understood in relation to the individual unit of husband and wife, but in relation to the universal plan God has for all persons.

---

[12] *Rule of Taizé*, 63.
[13] Ibid. 87.
[14] Ibid. 89.

Stability

The sad statistic is that more than half the marriages contracted in America now end in divorce. Christian marriages fare no better than non-Christian and, in fact, in denominations that have married clergy, clerical marriages fare a bit worse than the average when it comes to the divorce rate. This is but one clear indication that our society has a terrifying lack of stability. In the words of Esther de Waal, "we all need the certainty of knowing where we stand and where we belong."[15] In another place she says: "Everyone needs to feel at home, to feel earthed."[16] The choice for a stable life is intended to give this rootedness and commitment to persons and situations. Only some measure of stability fosters real growth in Christian life. We can only journey outward if we have a home from which we came and to which we can return.

In the monastic traditions that developed from Anthony and his anchorites (hermits), in the sayings of the desert fathers and mothers, we find a profound understanding of the value of stability. Let me give but two examples of this "desert wisdom." "Just as a tree cannot bear fruit if it is often transplanted, so neither can a monk bear fruit if he frequently changes his abode," and "stay in your cell, and your cell will teach you everything."[17] In cenobitic (communal) monastic communities stability has often meant lifelong residence within the boundaries of one monastery. But stability is to be understood in much wider than geographic terms. In marriage, shouldn't it become associated with lifelong residence within the boundary of one relationship, freely chosen and "cemented" by vows?

[15] Esther de Waal, "Freedom and Fullness of Life: The Rule and Vows in the Life of the Laity," a talk given at St. Mary's Abbey, Morristown, NJ, August 10, 1990.

[16] de Waal, *Seeking God*, 56.

[17] A particularly good collection of such sayings with a fine explanatory preface is Thomas Merton's *The Wisdom of the Desert* (New York: New Directions, 1960).

Situations clearly exist that are unliveable, and persons should not be asked to sacrifice themselves upon the altars of social respectability or ideal principles as, in previous generations, many were asked to do, and as sometimes still happens. Physical, emotional, psychological, or spiritual abuse are not part of God's plan for marriage and should not be condoned by the church. Just as marital poverty is not the injustice of economic oppression that some people are forced to live with, we are not now thinking about abusive relationships. There are worse things than divorce. Admitting this, it is still true that Christian marriage should be entered into and understood as "for keeps." Most of us choose our mates. The choice is a lifelong one; we are not to think we have an easy escape when "the honeymoon is over," when the realities of day-to-day life impinge upon our romantic fantasies, or when we "feel" we are no longer "in love." Most good marriages are emotionally tidal, "in and out," and almost every married person has rolled over one morning and thought, "I married *that!*"

But the locus of Christian life is not "below the belt"; it is at the foot of the cross. Our love for each other is not primarily something we "feel." It may, and usually does, begin there, but if it stays there we are condemning ourselves to marital (and emotional) adolescence. Mature love is something we will (volitional), something we choose to do, something we "act out" even (especially!) when we don't "feel like it." I dare say Jesus did not "feel like" dying on the cross. But God so loved that God gave, that is, acted, willed to act, for the good of others.

Older married couples do young people a great disservice if they pretend that marriage will be a trouble-free fairy tale of "happily ever after." Irritation, trials, troubles, temptations, routine, and just plain boredom are part of the picture even in good marriages. At best temporary, at worst coming in cycles, these difficulties may be understood as God's way of molding and maturing persons. We must be realistic in asserting that there will be problems in marriages, but we must understand that divorce is the last of the possible solutions to them. Amputating the hand is not the best cure for a broken fingernail.

Stability, however, does not mean *rigor mortis*. Stability in marriage should not prevent individual partners from growing. Indeed, it should encourage and nurture growth for both partners. Knowing one's self as loved gives one the courage to grow and to change. But, ironically, it is perhaps the growth of a spouse that is one of the greatest challenges to a marriage because growth implies change. If the wife grows in her understanding of her autonomy, how will her change affect her husband? If the husband grows in his capacity for relationships, will the wife be threatened?

In post-Vatican II monastic and religious communities monks and nuns grappled with serious changes and growth. Monks and nuns left their communities for periods of time to study, earn money for the community, serve the larger world. Married people have a lot to learn from the development of religious communities since Vatican II, some of it in the "do" category, and some of it in the "don't." Certainly flexibility is life-giving in relationship and community life. Without transgressing the vows they have made, perhaps married people need to view their stability in new and creative ways. Perhaps we need to think of our relationships with our husbands and wives as places we go out from and return to as we confront the world and face in it our God-given responsibilities to minister for the sake of Christ's kingdom. Stability in marriage might mean that one partner needs to be absent for a time, perhaps for further education or short-term mission work or a retreat. It might mean that who the primary breadwinner is would shift over the life of the marriage. Stability in marriage may mean flexibility of the kind that keeps a tree from being uprooted by a storm, or perhaps it is the "still, small voice" *in* the storm. Marital stability must embrace a dynamism that allows the partners mutually to be shaped in Christ's image. However a couple works with their stability (and no hard and fast rules apply, because each couple must work out the "what" and "how" for themselves), their understanding must presuppose the good of the other and the permanence and growth and flexibility that preserves the marriage itself.

The real purpose of stability understood in terms of relationship rather than of place is "the establishment of stability of the heart," which is the certainty "that God is everywhere, that we have no need to seek God elsewhere . . . because the kingdom of God begins within us."[18] Husbands and wives must understand that their ultimate stability is not in the spouse, but in God alone.

Hospitality

The last monastic virtue and Gospel value to be considered is the characteristic mark of the Benedictine tradition, hospitality. The root word *hospes*, from which we derive "hospice," "hospital," and "hospitable," means not only "host," but also "stranger" and "guest." To be hospitable implies receiving graciously as well as giving in a wonderful reciprocity between host and guest. Benedict's Rule teaches that "All who arrive as guests are to be welcomed like Christ," and "when the guests have been welcomed they should be led to prayer."[19] The essential practice of Benedictine houses is to receive each guest as Christ; the stranger is understood to be the Host. Thus humility and charity, not condescension, marks the reception of all guests, especially the poor and pilgrims. This simply mirrors what the gospels tell us of Jesus. He practiced universal table fellowship, welcomed sinners and ate with them (Luke 15:1-2), and, indeed, finally gave himself in the ultimate act of hospitality, his death on the cross.

It is impossible to say how many persons have become Christians because of the hospitality, the generous, cordial welcome, the offering of a pleasant, sustaining environment, the ready and willing receptivity of a Christian couple to others. Marriage should make people more open to others, more ready to include the solitary and lonely. My own life was dramatically shaped as a young, lonely graduate student by sustained hospitality from a loving family in my parish church. They took me in. That husband and wife were so secure in their love for each other, so confident about their love for their own children, that they could open their hearts and their home to another.

[18] de Waal, *Seeking God,* 60 and 62.
[19] David Parry, O.S.B., *Households of God* (London: Darton, Longman & Todd, 1980) 140.

In the current cultural climate our extension of hospitality must extend beyond our own "circle" or "class" or ethnic group and reach out to those who are different from us, and especially to those the world considers "unlovely"—the poor, the outcasts, the unknown and unwanted of the world. We must be ready to associate as widely as Jesus did with people in his own day, and be as persuasive in inviting strangers as was Lydia in including the traveling stranger, Paul (Acts 16:15). We have much to learn from other cultures about this matter of unquestioning generosity to strangers. Bedouin Arabs, for example, will feed guests from the desert sumptuously, knowing it will mean hungry days for themselves. And (dare I say it?) Christian hospitality must first and foremost be extended precisely to those we are tempted to call "enemy."

In an age of "sleep cheap" motels at every major intersection we are not called upon very frequently to shelter the traveler or pilgrim. And this diminishes us. I recall how much I learned eavesdropping on the adults in our home as my mother and father entertained missionaries on furlough and visiting preachers. In a very real sense all the people we encounter are pilgrims, persons on a journey to God. Everyone we meet is sent to us by God. Sometimes they know this and sometimes they don't. Here we need to learn quiet and creative ways to follow "step two" of Benedictine hospitality. After seeing to the physical needs of our guests, we must lead them to prayer, literally or metaphorically. We may not literally kneel with them, but our homes and hearts should create an environment that allows the presence of God to be felt. Brother David Steindl-Rast has written that even a "casual visitor to a monastery is apt to sense in some vague way that there is something special in that place." He suggests that having become more alert to God's mysterious presence, monks "learn to make things, design buildings, grow gardens, in such a way that others who use these things or live in these spaces are, in turn, made more mindful."[20]

---

[20] David Steindl-Rast, O.S.B., *A Listening Heart* (New York: Crossroad, 1984) 51–52.

Certainly this is also a worthy goal for a Christian home. The atmosphere of our homes should be different from that of the world around them, more orderly, more peaceful. For a period of our lives my husband and I had a variety of prayer and worship groups meeting around an altar in our living room. The Eucharist was regularly celebrated there. One of our great joys was when someone entered that room for the first time and said something like, "Oh, let's just stand here for a moment; this room has such a special feel." The hospitality we offer should not only minister to the physical needs of our guests and visitors, but should introduce them to the realm of that "special feel," the presence of God who is the source of our lives together, the source of our belonging.

It is so easy to bring the confusion and violence and noise of the street in with us, or worse, to create it ourselves in our homes. And such positive changes happen in the lives of families that choose another way, that choose to make of their homes not castles, but holy ground. I realize it is practically a heresy to suggest it, but one thing we can control is the television set. One of the easiest ways to exclude violent energy and to "end run" mindless consumption is simply to unplug the TV. We can teach our children not to scream at each other, and we can curb our own tendency to raise our voices in anger or frustration. We can create an environment that is hospitable for our own families and for others.

Conclusion

The primary vows of religious life, poverty, chastity, and obedience, and the special gifts of Benedictine monasticism, stability and hospitality, are also important in married life. As Louis Bouyer noted, "The giving up of all one's goods, of one's own body and, finally of one's own will, which is at the basis of monastic profession is in a certain way, equally at the basis of the marriage pact."[21] But the five great Christian virtues do not

---

[21] Louis Bouyer, *Introduction to Spirituality,* trans. Mary K. Ryan (New York: Desclee, 1961) 171.

touch the one that our country's most famous monk, Thomas Merton, thought was the most important. The vow of *conversatio morum*, conversion of life, is the essential monastic vow set forth in his book *The Monastic Journey*.[22] It is also the great and solemn vow that all serious Christians should be willing to make, the vow to turn their lives around, in Paul's terms to be transformed rather than conformed. In monastic formation this process begins early. It is often slow and difficult. In marriage, too, it is a slow and sometimes difficult journey from "mine" to "ours" to "God's." But I think it is the road we all must travel if our lives together are to show forth something of God's intentions for human beings.

In this regard the great Anglican spiritual teacher, Evelyn Underhill, lamented in her book *The Spiritual Life* that "we mostly spend our lives conjugating three verbs: to Want, to Have, and to Do." But the fundamental verb, she says, is to Be, and the Christian life should be anchored in Being by God, "soaked through and through by a sense of His reality and claim, and self-given to the great movement of His will."[23] The giving of the self to the will of God is the call to married persons, religious, and every Christian in whatever state of life.

Louis Bouyer made a profound observation about the spirituality of asceticism, the monastic way, that I think also holds true of the spirituality of Christian marriage and, indeed, of the life of all Christians. "Poverty . . . makes us free with regard to the world. Chastity makes us free with regard to the flesh. Obedience makes us free with regard to our will itself and its basic egoism."[24] Nearly sixteen hundred years earlier, Paul had sent the church at Galatia a similar message: "It is for freedom that Christ has set us free. Stand firm, then, and do not let yourselves be burdened again by a yoke of slavery" (Gal 5:1). The end of Christian life, whether lived in marriage, in religious orders, or

---

[22] Thomas Merton, *The Monastic Journey* (Kansas City: Sheed, Andrews and McMeel, 1977) 107.

[23] Evelyn Underhill, *The Spiritual Life* (New York: Harper, n.d.) 24, 36.

[24] Bouyer, *Introduction*, 135.

alone, is not slavery, but freedom. The task of Christian maturity is to grow into greater and greater freedom in Christ, to choose life and the great Giver of Life whose generosity is unbounded.

Questions for Discussion or Further Thought

1. How does the notion that monastic vows apply to Christian marriage strike you? Does this notion seem impractical? Intriguing? Explore your response to the idea.

2. Which of the vows seems most "translatable" to marriage? Which least? Why?

3. Would it be a useful exercise to write a "rule of life" for your marriage, or at least make notes toward such a "rule"? Remember the word "rule" is related to "trellis." It's not about a legalistic "enclosing," but about providing a framework for growth.

4. We have explored the idea that religious life is countercultural. How should Christian marriage also be countercultural?

Appendix

When I began to work on the talks for the Daughters of Wisdom in the Great Britain and Ireland Province, I began to notice and collect "re-writes" of the Beatitudes. During the course of my visits with the Sisters I was given several more "editions." They are often moving and creative. I include the best of them below.

I was usually given xerox copies without much in the way of sources. To the extent that I know the sources of these "re-writes," I have included them, and I would be happy for information that would allow for more complete citation.

Beatitudes of Reconciliation

Blessed are those who are willing to enter into the process of
    being healed,
    for they will become healers.
Blessed are those who recognize their own inner violence,
    for they will come to know nonviolence.
Blessed are those who can forgive self,
    for they will become forgivers.
Blessed are those who are willing to let go of selfishness and
    self-centeredness,

for they will become a healing presence.
Blessed are those who listen with compassion,
   for they will become compassionate.
Blessed are those who are willing to enter into conflict,
   for they will find resolutions.
Blessed are those who know their interdependence with all
      of creation,
   for they will become unifiers.
Blessed are those who live a contemplative life stance,
   for they will find God in all things.
Blessed are those who strive to live these beatitudes,
   for they will become reconcilers.

Sisters of St. Joseph, Concordia, Kansas

Beatitudes for Women

Blessed is she who suffers with the very young, the very old,
      and the very lonely,
   for she has compassion.
Blessed is she who greets the world with joy, laughter,
      and anticipation,
   for she has courage.
Blessed is she who speaks gently, lives humbly, and chooses
      to give freely,
   for she has dignity.
Blessed is she who listens and hears and extends her hands as
      a friend,
   for she has understanding.
Blessed is she who gives simply, loves deeply, and walks
      joyfully in life,
   for she has sincerity.
Blessed is she who lives intensely and sings life's alleluias,
   for she has awareness.

Blessed is she who has compassion and courage, freedom and
   dignity, understanding sincerity, and awareness,
   for she is a woman, a gift, a blessing.

Newark Archdiocesan Council of Catholic Women

The Smaller Beatitudes

Blessed are those who can laugh at themselves:
   they will have no end of fun.
Blessed are those who can tell a mountain from a molehill:
   they will be saved a lot of bother.
Blessed are those who know how to relax without looking
      for excuses:
   they are on the way to becoming wise.
Blessed are those who know when to be quiet and listen:
   they will learn a lot of new things.
Blessed are those who are sane enough not to take themselves
      seriously:
   they will be valued by those about them.
Happy are you if you can take small things seriously and face
      serious things calmly:
   you will go far in life.
Happy are you if you can appreciate a smile and forget
      a frown:
   you will walk on the sunny side of the street.
Happy are you if you can be kind in understanding the
   attitudes of others, even when the signs are unfavorable:
   you may be taken for a fool, but this is the price of charity.
Blessed are those who think before acting and pray before
      thinking:
   they will avoid many blunders.
Happy are you if you know how to hold your tongue
   and smile, even when people interrupt and contradict you
      or tread on your toes:
   the Gospel has begun to seep into your heart.
Above all, blessed are you who recognize the Lord in all whom
      you meet:

the light of truth shines in your life for you have found true wisdom.

Joseph Folliet (d. 1972)

Beatitudes of the Mentally Handicapped

Blessed are you who take time to listen to difficult speech,
   for you help us to know that as we persevere we can be
      understood.
Blessed are you who walk with us in public places and ignore
      the stares of strangers,
   for in your companionship we find havens of relaxation.
Blessed are you who are patient, never telling us to hurry,
   and more blessed are you who do not take our tasks from
      our hands to do them for us,
   for often we only need time rather than help.
Blessed are you who stand beside us as we enter new and
      untried ventures,
   for our failures will be outweighed by the times we surprise
      ourselves and you.
Blessed are you who ask for our help,
   for our greatest need is to be needed.
Blessed are you who help us with the graciousness of Christ,
   who did not bruise the reed or quench the flame,
   for often we need the help we cannot ask for.
Blessed are you when by your words and actions you assure
      us that the things that made
   us individuals are not in our uncoordinated movements,
   nor in our wounded nervous systems,
   nor in our difficulties, but in the God-given self which no
      infirmities can confine.
Rejoice and be exceedingly glad, and know that you give us
      reassurances that could never be spoken in words,
   for you deal with us as Christ dealt with all his children.

Beatitudes

Blessed are you, woman of prayer, worshiping God in spirit
and in truth,
for truth shall be added to you.
Blessed are you, woman of God, aflame with desire to know
and to accomplish the will of God,
for that will shall be shown to you.
Blessed are you, faithful religious, in love with your calling to
a community of faith,
for faith will sustain and renew your life.
Blessed are you, woman of integrity and self-knowledge,
for you shall neither deceive nor be deceived;
you shall neither be led into deception nor in any way be
allowed mediocrity.
You will avoid all moodiness and pettiness,
for you are a woman of integrity and self-knowledge.
Blessed are you, woman of this world, able to read the signs
of the times, in love with this world redeemed by God,
for in this world you will discern the action of a wonderful
God.
Blessed are you, woman of compassion, sensitive to the needs
and hurts of others,
for you shall be gentle and never harm or hurt.
Blessed are you, woman of attentive listening,
for you shall always hear, among the voices and above the
voices, the voice
of a loving God.
Blessed are you, woman of the spirit,
for you shall welcome and rejoice at the surprises of God.